On Educati

On Education

Conversations with Riccardo Mazzeo

Zygmunt Bauman

polity

First published in 2012 by Polity Press

Polity Press
65 Bridge Street
Cambridge CB2 1UR, UK

Polity Press
350 Main Street
Malden, MA 02148, USA

ISBN-13: 978-0-7456-6155-1
ISBN-13: 978-0-7456-6156-8(pb)

A catalogue record for this book is available from the British Library.

Typeset in 11 on 14 pt Sabon
by Servis Filmsetting Ltd, Stockport, Cheshire
Printed and bound in Great Britain by MPG Books Group Limited

The publisher has used its best endeavours to ensure that the URLs for external websites referred to in this book are correct and active at the time of going to press. However, the publisher has no responsibility for the websites and can make no guarantee that a site will remain live or that the content is or will remain appropriate.

Every effort has been made to trace all copyright holders, but if any have been inadvertently overlooked the publisher will be pleased to include any necessary credits in any subsequent reprint or edition.

For further information on Polity, visit our website: www.politybooks.com

Contents

Contents

I
Between mixophilia and mixophobia

Riccardo Mazzeo   I'd like to open this series of conversations by recalling the day almost two years ago when you first agreed to talk about education with me. It was a present you decided to offer to the 4,000 people who were going to gather in Rimini at our congress, The Quality of School Inclusion, in November 2009. You could not come to the congress because your absolute priority was to stay close to your wife, Janina, who was seriously ill. All the same, you allowed me and a cameraman to pay you a visit and record the precious video of your twenty-minute lecture.

You talked of the crisis of contemporary education, a very peculiar crisis because, probably for the first time in modern history, we are realizing that the differences among human beings and the lack of a universal model are going to be lasting. Living with foreigners, being exposed to the other, is nothing new but in the past it was believed that those who were 'alien' would sooner or later lose their 'difference' and be assimilated by accepting those universal values that were, in fact, *our* values. But nowadays this has changed: people who move to another country no longer desire to become like the natives, and the natives in turn have no wish to assimilate them.

So what happens in a city like London, where there are almost 180 diasporas who speak different languages and have different cultures and traditions? It is no longer a question of being tolerant, because tolerance is another face of discrimination; the challenge is at a higher level, about creating a feeling of solidarity.

There are two opposite reactions to the phenomenon in contemporary cities: mixophobia, the typical fear of being involved with foreigners, and mixophilia, the joy of being in a different and stimulating environment. The two conflicting trends are more or less as strong as each other: sometimes the first one prevails, sometimes the second. We cannot say which of them will carry the day, but in our globalized world, interconnected and interdependent, what we do in the streets, in primary and secondary schools, in the public places where we meet other people is extremely important not only for the future of the place we live in but for the future of the whole world.

As you know, we have been working to achieve school inclusion for more than twenty-five years, convinced that educating all children together, including those with special needs, is the best training children can receive for mixophilia. We were also able to take up the challenge because Italy is the only country in the world where full inclusion has been in force for almost forty years. But on the one hand inclusion has never been fully applied, and on the other hand some Italian politicians are trying to discredit public schooling, where 'communist teachers transmit ideas to our children that are different from the values we received from our parents' (to quote Berlusconi).

In your *Conversations* with Keith Tester (2001) you quoted Santayana's sentence 'Culture is a knife plunged into the future' and defined culture as 'a permanent revolution'. Do you think education needs to be fed not only with knowledge but also with critical thinking?

Zygmunt Bauman Nothing to take away from your words, Riccardo, and not much to add! I fully agree with you that conversion and assimilation, that early modern recipe for dealing with the presence of strangers, is not on the cards in the present context of a multicentred and multicultured world. The need to develop, to learn and to practise the art of living with strangers and their difference *permanently* and *daily* is inescapable for another reason as well: however hard state governments may try to prevent them, migrants are unlikely to stop knocking at a country's doors and those doors are unlikely to be kept closed.

'Europe needs immigrants': that was bluntly stated by Massimo D'Alema, currently president of the European Foundation for Progressive Studies, in *Le Monde* of 10 May 2011 – in direct dispute with, in his words, 'the two most active European pyromaniacs', Berlusconi and Sarkozy. Calculations to support D'Alema's verdict could hardly be simpler: there are 333 million Europeans today, but with the present average birth rate (still falling all over Europe) that number will shrink to 242 million in the next forty years. To fill that gap, at least 30 million newcomers will be needed – otherwise our European economy will collapse, together with our

3

cherished standard of living. 'Immigrants are an asset, not a danger', D'Alema concludes. And so the process of cultural *métissage* (hybridization), which the influx of newcomers is bound to trigger, is unavoidable; a mixing of cultural inspirations is a source of enrichment and an engine of creativity – for European civilization as much as for any other. All the same, there is only a thin line separating enrichment from a loss of cultural identity; for cohabitation between autochthons (indigenous inhabitants) and allochthons (those arrived from elsewhere) to be prevented from eroding cultural heritage, it needs to be based on respect for the principles underlying the European 'social contract'. . . the point is that this unwritten and unsigned contract needs to be respected by *both* sides!

How can one secure this respect, though, if recognition of the social and civil rights of 'new Europeans' is so stingily and haltingly offered, and proceeds at such a sluggish pace? Immigrants, for instance, currently contribute 11 per cent to Italian GNP, but they have no right to vote in Italian elections. In addition, no one can be truly certain how many newcomers there are with no papers or with counterfeit documents who actively contribute to the national product and thus to the nation's well-being. 'How can the European Union', asks D'Alema, all but rhetorically, 'permit a situation in which political, economic and social rights are denied to a substantive part of the population, without undermining our democratic principles?' And since citizen duties come in a package deal with citizen rights, again, in principle, can one seriously expect the newcomers to embrace, respect, support and defend those 'principles underlying the European social contract'? Our politicians muster electoral support by blaming immigrants for their genuine or putative reluctance to 'integrate' with the autochthons' standards – while doing all they can, and promising to do yet more, to put those standards beyond the allochthons' reach. On the way, they discredit or erode the very standards they claim to be protecting against foreign invasion. . .

The big question, a quandary more likely to determine the future of Europe than any other, is which one of the two contending 'facts of the matter' will eventually (but without too much delay) come out on top: the life-saving role played by immigrants in a fast-ageing Europe, a role few if any politicians thus far dare to emblazon on their banners; or the power-abetted and power-assisted rise in xenophobic sentiments eagerly recycled into electoral votes? The official ministerial pronouncements and statistics of voting intentions suggest one tendency, while the daily habits and slow but relentless 'subterranean' changes in life's setting and logic at the grassroots seem to point in another direction.

After their dazzling victory in the provincial election in Baden-Württemberg – leaving the social democrats trailing and, for the first time in the history of the Bundesrepublik, putting one of their own, Winfried Kretschmann, at the head of a provincial government – the German Greens, and notably Daniel Cohn-Bendit, are begining to ponder the possibility that the German Chancellery in Berlin could turn green as soon as 2013. Who will make that history in their name? Cohn-Bendit has little doubt: Cem Özdemir, their sharp-minded and clear-headed, dynamic, charismatic, widely admired and revered co-leader re-elected a few months ago by 88 per cent of the party members who voted. Until his eighteenth birthday, Özdemir held a Turkish passport; then he, a young man already deeply engaged in German and European politics, chose German citizenship because of the harassment to which Turkish nationals were bound to be exposed whenever they tried to enter the United Kingdom or hop over the border to neighbouring France. One wonders: who, in present-day Europe, are the advance messengers of Europe's future? Europe's most active pair of pyromaniacs, or Daniel Cohn-Bendit? Not being a prophet and believing that history is made by people and doesn't exist until it has been made by them, I can't answer that question. But it will have to be answered, in words as much as in deeds, by all of us alive at present. And it will be answered – by our choices.

For more than forty years of my life in Leeds I have watched from my window as children returned home from the nearby secondary school. Children seldom walk alone; they prefer walking in groups of friends. That habit has not changed. And yet what I see from my window has changed over the years. Forty years ago, almost every group was 'single colour'; nowadays, almost none of them are . . .

2

José Saramago: ways of being happy

Riccardo Mazzeo Reading what you say about the need, if the European 'social contract' is to be really effective, that autochthons and allochthons *both* respect it, and what you add in the following paragraph underlining politicians' manoeuvres to sabotage the possibility of immigrants really reaching the standards needed to be 'integrated', I recalled the words José Saramago said to some friends about the economic crisis a few days before he died. He said that we all, governments and citizens, know what is needed to get out of the crisis, but being willing to do it is far from easy. And we are not inclined to take that step because in order to change our life we would have to change our way of living and this is something we usually ask to others to do, certainly not ourselves. For Saramago, the absolute priority is the human being, the other who is the same as I and has the right to say: 'I'.

In his last *Caderno*, day 17 of July 2009, Saramago writes that each of us has a few stains of emigration on his or her family tree, either one's father or one's father's father. Many Portuguese were drowned trying to swim across the River Bidasoa to get from Spain to France, a place they imagined as a paradise. The survivors had to submit to menial jobs, bear humiliation, learn unfamiliar languages, and suffer social isolation, but they proudly built a future for their descendants. Some of these people haven't lost and haven't wanted to lose, the memory of the bad times, and we must be grateful to those who successfully safeguarded the respect due to their past. A majority, by contrast, feel ashamed of having been ignorant and poor, and behave as if a decent life could begin for them only on the gorgeous day when they could at last buy their first car. The person who used to be exploited, and has forgotten it, will exploit other people; the person who used to be looked down on, and pretends to have forgotten it, will now do the same; and here they all are together, flinging stones at the people arriving at the bank of the Bidasoa. 'Verily I tell you', Saramago concludes, 'that there are ways of being happy that are simply hateful.'

Both you and Saramago have sometimes been accused of being pessimistic about the future of the world (because people don't understand, I suppose, that you state the preconditions for saving the world), but I see that Saramago was writing the Charter (Carta) of the Duties when he died, and it seems to me that drawing up such a document has to imply the word 'trust'. And to talk about you, I think of the last sentence of your first answer, like a beautiful poem, and filled with trust.

Zygmunt Bauman   You bring me back to sombre and sad aspects of our being-in-the-world; and, alas, you are right again: 'a person who used to be exploited, and has forgotten it, will exploit other people; the person who used to be looked down on, and pretends to have forgotten it, will now do the same'. . . I have not yet found, though I keep looking for, a case of victimization that has ennobled its victims instead of stripping them of humanity (Janina concluded from her own cruel lessons that remaining human under inhuman conditions is the most difficult of feats). The memory of one's own suffering, and even the present-day phenomenon of a contrived, second-hand memory of sufferings not experienced first-hand, does not make people more generous, kind or sensitive to other people's pains. On the contrary, it prompts the descendants of victims to be cruel to the descendants of the perpetrators of cruelty, and it is used as a certificate of pre-payment for one's own insensitivity and a blank cheque for one's own inhumanity. Violence, inhumanity, humiliation and victimization set off what Gregory Bateson called 'schismogenetic chains', genuine Gordian knots ruggedly resistant to being broken or cut however artful the sword you brandish. Saramago focused on Portugal, the country closest to his heart, but the tide of xenophobia rising in Portugal is not an exception, but a rule. Once they turn into importers of labour, almost all countries that previously exported labour (such as Ireland, Italy, France, Sweden, Norway, Denmark or the Netherlands) manifest the same inclination. We can watch, thus far helplessly, a tide of neo-tribal sentiments swelling from Copenhagen to Rome and from Paris to Prague, magnified and beefed up by the deepening alerts and fears of the 'enemy at the gate' and 'fifth columns', resulting in a 'besieged fortress' mentality manifested in the fast rising popularity of securely locked borders and doors firmly shut.

3
Gregory Bateson and his third level of education

Riccardo Mazzeo Thanks for mentioning Bateson's 'schismogenetic chains', admirably explained in your 2008 book *Does Ethics Have a Chance in a World of Consumers?* I had been impressed by Bateson's *Steps to an Ecology of Mind,* on which Richard Kopp based another book, *Metaphor Therapy: Using Client-Generated Metaphors in Psychotherapy*, which I edited and translated into Italian in 1998, finding it very useful in my activity as a counsellor. The principle of the metaphor as 'connecting structure' is vividly evidenced by the wonderful metaphors contained in your work, and the influence of Bateson's life on his theory makes me think of you, too. Your own dramatic experience in 1968 brought you to your second life in Leeds and induced you, thirty years later in Prague on the occasion of your *honoris causa* degree, to accept Janina's advice not to choose either the British national anthem, 'because in Great Britain you remained in a way a foreigner', or the Polish one, 'because Poland had deprived you of Polish citizenship', but to opt instead for the European national anthem: 'Alle Menschen werden Brüder'. You mentioned this episode of your life in *Identity*, with Benedetto Vecchi, and you devoted the last chapter of *Liquid Modernity* to the hard but fruitful condition of being uprooted and forced to get the hang of a new world: as Sartre stated, we are not what others make of us, we are what we do with what others have made of us.

Gregory Bateson had an awkward father, William Bateson, who was also the famous father of genetics. His eldest brother died in World War I, when he was a little boy, and this is something that can happen. But his other brother, Martin, committed suicide on the day of the eldest brother's birthday, when Gregory was eighteen, and so their father's expectations for a son to reincarnate him as a genius fell entirely on the only one remaining, Gregory.

Gregory Bateson's ambivalence in trying to differentiate himself from his father and the impossibility of giving up his true interest in biology may have fuelled his later discovery of the 'double bind', an approach that changed psychiatry; his internal psychic conflict helped to drive his discovery of schismogenesis among the Iatmul, in New Guinea. He realized that schismogenesis was not the only possible option: his research in Bali, Indonesia, revealed that this model was not in force there, but the schismogenetic process had unfolded within his personality, cropped up in his intimate relations (after his marriage to Margaret Mead, he married again twice) and it remained the focus of his interest in culture and politics. We are all immensely grateful to Bateson for his insightful studies, but I mention his painful relationship with his father to introduce

the protagonists of our conversation, children and the
tougher and tougher mission of these liquid times: their
education.

Zygmunt Bauman Bateson, in my reckoning, was
indeed one of the brightest, most creative and most
original minds in anthropology of the last century. His
concept of schismogenetic chains embraced two different kinds: symmetrical, in which the competing sides
take a 'one-upmanship' stance, as in an arms race, for
instance; and complementary, when the attitudes on
either side of a conflict are mutually opposite and recip-
rocally reinforcing, as in the case of arrogance versus
submissiveness, when each time one stance is tightened
it intensifies and exacerbates the other. Although dis-
tilled from fieldwork experience in New Guinea, the
concept throws enormous light on the dynamics of com-
petitive behaviour in all kinds of human interaction – by
no means confined to 'primitive' cultures or to one-to-
one, face-to-face situations.

Another priceless contribution of Bateson, still more
intimately related to our topic, is his distinction between
three levels of education. The lowest is the transfer of
information to be memorized. The second, 'deutero-
learning', is aimed at the mastering of a 'cognitive
frame' into which information acquired or encountered
in the future can be absorbed and incorporated. But
there is also a third level, imparting the ability to dis-
assemble and rearrange the prevailing cognitive frame
or to dispose of it completely, without a replacing
element. That third level was viewed by Bateson as a
pathological, in fact a counter-educational phenomenon
(well, this was the time when Erik Erikson considered

fluidity of identity to be a psychological sickness. . .).
And yet, while the lowest of Bateson's three levels has
since fallen out of use – with memory being transfered
from the brain to electronic discs, USB sticks and servers
– what Bateson treated as a cancer rather than healthy
tissue has turned into the norm in the teaching/learning
process (a similar reversal has taken place in the status
of identities. . .).

I believe this is one of the most remarkable departures
in the setting of education, and potentially also in its
methodologies – and, indeed, in the very meaning of
knowledge and the fashion of its production, distribution, acquisition, assimilation and utilization. I am sure
we will be returning to these issues over and over again
in our conversation. . .

4

From closure of mind to 'permanent revolution'

Riccardo Mazzeo In Italy, it is unusual for a book talking about schooling to reach the top of the best-seller list and to remain there for months. This is what happened to Paola Mastrocola's book called *We'll Go Our Own Way: Essay on the Freedom Not to Continue Studying*. In the book, the author, a high school teacher and pleasant novelist, attacks Don Milani (author of the very famous *Letter to a Teacher*, published in 1967) and Gianni Rodari (who wrote *The Grammar of Imagination* in 1973). Don Milani is renowned in Italy because he was one of the first to stress the importance of education for all the children who, because of their disadvantaged social position, didn't have the tools to succeed in schools. Gianni Rodari, on the other hand, insisted on the importance of creativity and of learning through play. Moreover, Mastrocola criticizes our most prominent linguist and former Minister of Education, Tullio De Mauro, for envisioning an education that valorizes 'practical, concrete and immediately applicable knowledge'. Talking about her ideal student,

Mastrocola describes him or her as the one student in twenty-five who, when questioned, 'repeats everything I told them'. Despite her ability to catch the discontent of teachers and parents – understandably tired of seeing their kids captured by Facebook and by all sort of short-lived trends – I was personally very surprised by how well received this book was.

Mastrocola treats school education, where 1 million people are committed to teaching at their best, as a glasshouse where the students' task is simply to swallow a set of notions and then spit them out. I think there is a double simplification at the root of this position. On one hand, the author, a teacher with a frustrated wish to have students memorize her lessons (and I think having to teach Torquato Tasso, one of our most boring canonized writers, doesn't make her task easy), has come to think that the only solution is to remove all those who don't measure up to her standards. The second simplification involves her readers, who are obviously tired of seeing their own teaching efforts fail and thus are eager to adopt fast and clear-cut measures.

Zygmunt Bauman It took more than two millennia, from the time the ancient Greek sages invented the notion of *paidea*, before the idea of 'lifelong education' changed from an oxymoron (a contradiction in terms) into a pleonasm (akin to 'buttery butter' or 'metallic iron'). That remarkable transformation occurred quite recently, in the last few decades, as a result of the radically accelerated pace of change in the social setting of both the principal actors of education, the teachers and the learners alike.

The moment ballistic missiles start moving, their

direction and distance of their travel have already been
decided by the shape and position of the gun barrel and
the amount of gunpowder in the shell; one can calculate
with little or no error the spot where the missile will
land, and can choose that spot by shifting the barrel
or changing the dose of gunpowder. These qualities
of ballistic missiles made them ideal weapons to use in
positional warfare – when the targets stayed dug into
their trenches or bunkers and the missiles were the sole
bodies on the move.

The same qualities make them useless, however,
once targets invisible to the gunner start to move –
particularly if they move faster than missiles can fly, and
even more so if they move erratically, in an unpredictable fashion that plays havoc with all the preliminary
calculations of the required trajectory. A smart, intelligent missile is needed then, a missile that can change
its direction in full flight depending on changing circumstances, one that can immediately spot the target's
movements, learn from them whatever needs to be
learned about the target's current direction and speed,
and extrapolate from the information gathered the spot
where their trajectories will cross. These smart missiles cannot suspend, let alone finish the gathering and
processing of information as they travel – as their target
keeps on moving and changing direction and speed, the
plotting of the point of encounter needs to be constantly
updated and corrected.

We can say that smart missiles follow a strategy of
'instrumental rationality', though in its liquidized, fluid
version, so to speak; that is, they drop the assumption
that the end is given, steady and immovable for the duration, and so only the means need to be calculated and

manipulated. Even smarter missiles won't be confined to a preselected target at all but will choose the targets as they go. They will rather be guided by an assessment of the most they can achieve given their technical capacities, and which of potential targets around they are best equipped to hit. This would be, we can say, a case of 'instrumental rationality' in reverse: targets are selected as the missile travels, and it is the available means that decide which 'end' will be eventually selected. In such case, the 'smartness' of the flying missile and its effectiveness will benefit if its equipment is of a rather 'generalistic' or 'uncommitted' nature, unfocused on any specific category of ends, not overly adjusted to the hitting a particular kind of target.

Smart missiles, unlike their ballistic elder cousins, *learn as they go*. So what they need to be supplied with initially is the *ability* to learn, and learn fast. This is obvious. What is less visible, however, though no less crucial than the skill of quick learning, is the ability to instantly *forget* what was learned before. Smart missiles wouldn't be smart were they not able to 'change their minds' or revoke their previous 'decisions' without a second thought or regret. . . They should not overly cherish the information they have acquired and on no account should they develop a *habit* of behaving in the way that information suggested. All the information they acquire ages rapidly; instead of providing reliable guidance it may lead them astray unless it can be promptly dismissed. What the 'brains' of smart missiles must never forget is that the knowledge they acquire is eminently *disposable*, good only until further notice and of only temporary usefulness, and that the warrant of success is not to overlook the moment when acquired knowledge is of no use any longer and needs to be thrown away, forgotten and replaced.

Philosophers of education of the solid modern era saw teachers as launchers of ballistic missiles and instructed them on how to make sure their products stayed strictly on the predesigned course determined by the momentum of the initial trigger. And no wonder; ballistic missiles at the early stages of the modern era were the topmost achievement of human technical inventiveness. They flawlessly served whoever wished to conquer and master the world as it then was; as Hilaire Belloc confidently declared, referring to the African natives, 'Whatever happens, we have got the Maxim Gun, and they have not' (the Maxim Gun, let's recall, was a machine to launch great numbers of ballistic bullets in a short time, and was effective only if there were very many such bullets at hand). As a matter of fact, though, that vision of the teacher's task and the pupil's destiny was much older than the idea of the 'ballistic missile' and the modern era that invented it – as is testified by an ancient Chinese proverb, preceding the advent of modernity by two millennia but still quoted by the Commission of the European Communities in support of its programme for 'lifelong learning' at the threshold of the twenty-first century: 'When planning for a year, plant corn. When planning for a decade, plant trees. When planning for life, train and educate people.' It is only with the entry into liquid modern times that the ancient wisdom lost its pragmatic value and people concerned with learning and the promotion of learning known under the name of 'education' had to shift their attention from ballistic to smart missiles.

Professor John Kotter at Harvard Business School has advised his readers to avoid being entangled in long-term employment of the 'tenure track' sort; indeed, developing institutional loyalty and becoming too deeply engrossed and emotionally engaged in any given job, swearing a long-term, not to mention a lifelong commitment, is ill advised when 'business concepts, product designs, competitor intelligence, capital equipment and *all kinds of knowledge* have shorter credible life spans'.[1]

If premodern life was a daily rehearsal of the infinite duration of everything except mortal life, liquid modern life is a daily rehearsal of universal transience. What the denizens of the liquid modern world soon find out is that nothing in that world is bound to last, let alone forever. Objects recommended today as useful and indispensable tend to 'become history' well before they have had time to settle down and turn into a need or a habit. Nothing is believed to be here for ever, nothing seems to be irreplaceable. Everything is born with the brand of imminent death and emerges from the production line with a 'use-by date' printed or presumed. The construction of new buildings does not start unless permissions have been issued to demolish them when the time comes to pull them apart, as it surely will, and contracts are not signed unless their duration is fixed or it is made easy to terminate them on demand. Few if any commitments last long enough to reach the point of no return, and it is only by accident that decisions, all deemed to be binding only 'for the time being', stay in force. Every thing that is born or made, human or not, is merely until-further-notice and dispensable. A spectre hovers over the denizens of the liquid modern world and

---

1   John Kotter, *The New Rules* (New York: Dutton, 1995), p.159, emphasis added.

all their labours and creations: the spectre of superfluity. Liquid modernity is a civilization of excess, redundancy, waste and waste disposal. In a succinct and pithy formulation by Riccardo Petrella, current global trends direct 'economies towards the production of the ephemeral and volatile – through the massive reduction of the lifespan of products and services – and of the precarious (temporary, flexible and part-time jobs)'.[2]

The great Italian sociologist Alberto Melucci used to say that 'we are plagued by the fragility of the presentness which calls for a firm foundation where none exists'. And so, 'when contemplating change, we are always torn between desire and fear, between anticipation and uncertainty'.[3] Uncertainty means *risk*: the undetachable companion of all action and a sinister spectre haunting the compulsive decision-makers and choosers by necessity that we have been since, as Melucci pithily put it, 'choice became a destiny'.

As a matter of fact, to say 'became' is not entirely correct, because humans have been choosers as long as they have been humans. But it can be said that at no other time has the necessity to make choices been so deeply felt and has choosing become so poignantly self-conscious, conducted under conditions of painful yet incurable uncertainty, of a constant threat of 'being left behind' and of being excluded from the game, with return barred for failure to live up to the new demands. What separates the present-day agony of choice from the discomforts that have always tormented the *homo*

2 Riccardo Petrella, 'Une machine infernale', *Le Monde Diplomatique*, June 1997, p. 17.
3 Alberto Melucci, *The Playing Self: Person and Meaning in the Planetary Society* (Cambridge: Cambridge University Press, 1996), pp. 43ff.

eligens, the 'man choosing', is the discovery or suspicion that there are no preordained rules and universally approved objectives to be followed which could thereby absolve the choosers of the adverse consequences of their choices. Any reference points and guidelines that seem trustworthy today are likely to be debunked tomorrow as misleading or corrupt. Allegedly rock-solid companies are unmasked as figments of accountants' imagination. What is 'good for you' today may be reclassified as your poison tomorrow. Apparently firm commitments and solemnly signed agreements may be overturned overnight. And promises, or most of them, seem to be made solely to be betrayed and broken. There seems to be no island stable and secure from the tides. To quote Melucci once more, 'we no longer possess a home; we are repeatedly called upon to build and then rebuild one, like the three little pigs of the fairy tale, or we have to carry it along with us on our backs like snails'.

In a world like this, one is therefore compelled to take life bit by bit, as it comes, expecting each bit to be different from the ones before, calling for different knowledge and skills. Gregory Bateson, one of the most insightful anthropologists of all time, famous for his ability to spot still incipient, inchoate and barely visible cultural trends, noted (more than half a century ago!) the imminent 'educational revolution'. There are three levels in teaching/learning, he wrote. At the first and lowest level, it is just as Paola Mastrocola would wish it to be: pupils repeating word for word what their teachers tell them: 'rote learning', memorizing, building fortifications against any contravening or just out-of-place information, therefore viewed as 'irrelevant'. The production of typical 'ballistic missiles', we can say. At a higher, second level, Bateson places the formation of cognitive frames and predispositions that enable orientation in an as yet unfamiliar situation, as well as the absorption, assimilation and incorporation of new knowledge. This, we can say, is the kind of teaching/learning aimed at the production of 'smart missiles' (nowadays ever more often dubbed 'intelligent'). There is, however, Bateson suggested, a third, still higher level of learning, mastering the moment when 'anomalous data' become too numerous to be dismissed as aberrations and neglected, and when a radical overhaul of the cognitive frame is called for to accommodate and 'make sense' of them. Somewhat later, Thomas Kuhn called that moment a 'scientific revolution' and suggested that all progress in knowledge is bound to stumble from one such revolution to another. I would say that today we are all cast in a perpetually 'revolutionary' condition. Our knowledge is in a state of 'permanent revolution'. As far as I can gather, under such conditions Mastrocola's model of teaching is a recipe for disabling instead of enabling youngsters about to join the company of grown-ups. And the one invariable purpose of education, was, is and will always remain the preparation of those youngsters for life according to the realities they are bound to enter. To be prepared, they need instruction: 'practical, concrete and immediately applicable knowledge', to use Tullio De Mauro's expression. And to be 'practical', quality schooling needs to provoke and propagate openness, not closure of mind.

5
Oak trees and ridiculously minute acorns

Riccardo Mazzeo As you asserted at the Festival dell'Economia in Trento, if the world is out of joint and parents compensate for their lack of care and attention to their children by purchasing top-notch merchandise; if they themselves have abandoned the time for solitary reflection in favour of multitasking on the internet; if they have forgotten the 'art of life' about which you talked in the book you wrote with the same title; if they don't understand that a love relationship requires time, care and flexibility, and instead prefer to break up their marriage rather than tending it like a plant, with a little water every day; if adults rely exclusively on instrumental reason and no longer have the capacity to think critically. . . how can we expect children and students to be able to do so, given the morally polluted air they breathe and the examples they see around them?

Zygmunt Bauman Vaclav Havel, no stranger, as you know, to a world of overwhelming and apparently indomitable pressures and coercions, with a life spent alternately inside walled prisons and in prisons without walls, drew the following lesson from his experience: if you want to change the world, you first need to know what songs the people are ready to sing (being a poet himself, Havel was inclined to draw his metaphors from the world of the arts). But, he added immediately, there is no way of knowing what sort of songs people will fancy singing next year. . .

Homo sapiens stands out from the rest of animal creation by being underdefined and underdetermined, being thereby condemned to transcendence, to defiance of the status quo, to reaching 'beyond' and 'above'. Our distant ancestors, writers of the Bible, were already aware of that plight when they laid down the injunctions 'with labour you shall win your food' and 'in labour you shall bear children' as the *only* binding instructions God gave to Adam and Eve, respectively, in sending them off into the world they were to inhabit. . .

The form of life practised by each and every one of us is a combined result of fate (something we can do little about, even though it is, at least in part, a summary product of past human choices) and character (something we can work on, reform and recompose). Fate delineates the set of feasible options, but it is character that chooses between them, picking up some and rejecting others. There is no situation that does not contain more than one option (that truly universal rule applies even to the inmates of concentration camps, that embodiment of ultimate disablement), and so there is no 'situation without choice' – no situation when something else could not be done in place of what is being done; and there is no choice, no decision and no action without an alternative.

The conviction that has kept me seeking, thinking and writing over the years is that in order to make proper use of freedom of choice (however reduced) we need precisely to be aware of the range of options offered by 'fate' (the unchosen historical moment in which we have to act), and of the set of alternative actions (or rather the ways of acting) from which we can choose. Describing successive conditions in which 'fate' has cast us, I have tried (and still go on trying) to find out and spell out what chances *and* threats specific conditions potentially contain. Because of my uncannily long life, I have had the opportunity to perform such an operation on quite a few sharply distinct conditions; and I have failed to come across a form of life which lacked either of the two. The present form of life, one I have been struggling to take stock of in the last ten years or so (the 'liquid modern', deregulated and individualized society of consumers formed in an increasingly globalized setting), is no exception.

And so there is much room for concern, but none for despair. Your question as to whether – given the presently prevailing and seemingly overwhelming pressures, fads and foibles – we may still hope or expect our children and students to behave differently from the way the majority currently do, my answer is 'yes'. If it is true (and it is) that each set of circumstances contains some chances alongside its dangers, it is also true that each is as pregnant with rebellion as it is with conformity. Let's never forget that each majority started from being a tiny, invisible and unnoticeable minority. And that even hundred-year-old oak trees have grown from ridiculously minute acorns. . .

6
Looking for a genuine 'cultural revolution'

Riccardo Mazzeo I read today (17 July 2011) that two of the charismatic leaders you have mentioned in your answers, Cem Özdemir and Vaclav Havel, have just been united in their refusal to permit the Quadriga prize to be awarded to Vladimir Putin as 'an exemplary model of people who work for the common good': the association Werkstatt Deutschland had to backtrack. It is no surprise: they are heroes and Putin could be celebrated in that way only in George Orwell *1984*; but it acts as a confirmation that as soon as you said 'There is no situation without choice', both Özdemir and Havel immediately rebelled against an injustice. The association of these ideas brings back to my mind Nazim Hikmet, who was Turkish, like Özdemir, and who was a poet, a revolutionary and (for many years) a prisoner like Havel. I chose a poem by Hikmet for the announcement of my wedding, a poem pressing for life to be taken seriously, to the point that 'when you are eighty you will plant an olive tree'. It is an image intrinsically contained in your conclusion that we are still allowed to hope because 'even hundred-year-old oak trees have grown from ridiculously minute acorns'. How could endurance, planning skills, long-term wishes and all the human qualities that have made human beings capable of building a better life disappear?

One of your disciples, Mauro Magatti, has written a prominent book, *Libertà immaginaria* (Imaginary Freedom), with the subtitle 'The Illusions of Techno-nihilist Capitalism', in which he illustrates the damage done by philosophical deconstructionism: 'The shift from the conception of nature as order to a vision in which the idea of an infinite process of construction and deconstruction prevails is the first step to start from to smash all the bricks modern thought was built with.'[4] Here Bateson's third level is at work: only the people who are able to jump from one opportunity to another, able to perform in conditions of uncertainty, able to forget once important but now irrelevant notions, only those people survive and are successful (until further orders).

Magatti describes the new scenario: 'There is no longer centre and periphery, high or low, right or wrong: Techno-Nihilist Capitalism tends to subsume everything, including what is produced at its margins and even what opposes it. There is no more counter-culture because "everything is cultural production". Counterculture actually constitutes a form of novelty which enriches variety and as such is incorporated into the system.'[5] If the new system in force eats up, digests

---

4   Mauro Magatti, *Libertà immaginaria. Le illusioni del tecno-capitalismo tecno-nichilista* (Milan: Einaudi, 2009), p. 102.
5   Ibid., p. 109.

and capitalizes every intervention of resistance, starting from today, what can we do?

Zygmunt Bauman You've put your finger on perhaps the crucial obstacle to the effectiveness of the consistent and the coherent in our market mediated and guided society of consumers: the omnivorous capacity of consumer markets, their uncanny ability to capitalize on any and every human problem, anxiety, apprehension, pain or suffering – their ability to turn every protest and every impact of a 'countervailing force' to its advantage and profit. On the other hand, with markets in full control of channels of re-presentation, publicity and communication, critical and opposition forces have little choice but to play according to market rules and – obliquely but no less strongly – thereby endorse and reinforce market rule.

In his recently published study *Redefining Prosperity*, Professor Tim Jackson blames the greed of profit only indirectly, singling out as the main culprit 'our culture founded on continuing appetite for novelty – which is the symbolic aspect of objects'. It is because of that forcefully trained and already deeply ingrained appetite that we find ourselves continually encouraged and inclined to behave egotistically and materialistically – this kind of behaviour being indispensable to keep our kind of economy, the consumerist economy, going. We are prodded, forced or cajoled to buy and to spend – to spend what we have and to spend what we don't have but hope to earn in the future. Unless that undergoes a radical change, the chances of effective dissidence and liberation from the market's dictates are minimal. The odds against are overwhelming.

Nothing short of a genuine 'cultural revolution' will do. However limited the powers of the present education system look, and it is itself increasingly subject to the consumerist game, it still has enough transformative powers left to be counted among the promising factors for such revolution.

7

Depravation is the cleverest strategy of deprivation

Riccardo Mazzeo Perhaps one of the reasons for the urgency of the 'cultural revolution' you wish and believe possible is, at least in Italy, the so-called 'subcultural hegemony' (from the book by Massimiliano Panarari with the same title).[6] It refers to the deliberate use of the methods described by Antonio Gramsci as permitting the hegemony of the people through access to culture, reversed into analogous methods used to make people reluctant to engage with culture and critical thinking thanks to massive exposure to never-ending TV entertainment with more and more girls wearing low-necked dresses, the telling of dirty funny stories, the depressing tendency (skilfully cultivated and induced) towards what you have called 'emotional striptease', and the triumph of tabloids filled with gossip (TV channels and tabloids are owned by our premier, and the brains of the manoeuvre is Alfonso Signorini, a 'real' but bought

6 M. Panarari, *L'egemonia sottoculturale. L'Italia da Gramsci al gossip* (Milan: Einaudi, 2010).

intellectual, the director of the two best-selling tab-loids). A second reason is the disheartening belittlement of school. In an affluent society the job of the teacher is frequently disregarded, because in the wealthiest countries this long-term investment for one's children would require an active participation that parents, too busy and too caught in the consuming trap, don't want to make.

It is instead from school that we should start again. A contribution to this revaluation has recently arrived with the book on 'School Days' edited by Tullio De Mauro and Dario Ianes.[7] De Mauro quotes Ecclesiastes to describe teachers: 'Let us now praise famous men/ men of little showing./ For their work continueth/ and this work continueth/ broad and deep continueth,/ greater than their knowing.' And Ianes, for his part: 'In this moment of the night, those who still believe in it are writing a unit for some pupils or looking on the internet for updated news for the classroom. Those who still believe in it carry their jobs even into the bathroom, as many other professionals do, of course, but their job appears with a face, a name'. Twenty teachers (from kindergarten to high school, including two headmasters) offer their testimony and some talk of 'the resources they find in themselves, that they patiently develop day after day, instead of just waiting for them to appear, swearing or complaining'.

I have personally known a lot of teachers and I have perceived a genuine interest and even a passion for their

---

7 T. De Mauro and D. Ianes (eds), *Giorni di scuola. Pagine di diario di chi ci crede ancora* (School Days: Journal Pages of Those Who still Believe In It) (Trento: Erickson, 2011).

work, so first of all I think we should respect them, but
obviously this is not enough. In Italy we have almost
100 per cent success until the end of secondary school;
then the success dramatically falls and more than 30 per
cent drop out before the high school diploma. Some of
the fugitives go off to attend shifty private schools, but
every year 120,000 young people swell the ranks of the
neets (not in education, employment or training) and
there Italian neets among 15 to 19 year olds are now
more than 2 million. So it's clear that something heavy
happens during this transition. What do you think
about that?

Zygmunt Bauman Depravation is the cleverest strategy of deprivation. The shifting of attention (through
temptation and seduction), and thereby also 'life rel-
evance', away from acquiring skills to fishing for sensual
impressions, which you so expertly spot and expose in
the diet of TV, is the technique of depravation produc-
ing the legions of 'neets' you bewail. This is indeed an
insidious technique – one that renders continuous deprivation pleasurable, and makes servitude something that
is perceived and felt as freedom of choice. . .

And another point: people like Alfonso Signorini
would probably point out that we should be wary of
blaming the messenger for the content and the consequences of the message. Television or the tabloid
press does not knead us into a different shape; it rather
draws to the surface, reveals and puts on display what
is 'inside' us, already preprocessed by the form of life
into which we – not by choice – have been cast. The
form of life into which the young generation of today
has been born, so that it knows no other, is a society

of consumers and a 'nowist' – restless and perpetually changing – culture, promoting the cult of novelty and random chance. In such a society and such a culture, we smart at the excessive supply of everything, of the objects of desire as much as the objects of knowledge, and at the mind-boggling speeds of the new objects coming in and the old falling out. The resonance between the TV schedules (a whirlwind of low-necked dresses and emotional stripteases) and the way our form of life has trained and drilled us to feel and desire is measured by TV ratings. Watching TV is after all not obligatory, and switching it off is not punishable. At least in this part of our decision-making we still have freedom of choice. Not switching it off is as much a decision as switching it on. Or so it seems. . .

'There is far too much information around,' Thomas Hylland Eriksen observes in his *Tyranny of the Moment*. 'A crucial skill in information society consists in protecting oneself against the 99.99 per cent of the information offered that one does not want.' We can say that the line separating a meaningful message, the ostensible object of communication, from its acknowledged adversary and obstacle, namely the background noise, has all but disappeared. There is cut-throat competition for any time consumers' have still lying fallow, for the tiniest gaps between moments of consumption that still might be stuffed with more information. Suppliers hope that some of those at the receiving end of the communication channel, in the course of their desperate searches for the bits of information they do need might by chance come across the bits they don't yet need but the suppliers want them to absorb, and then might be sufficiently impressed to pause or slow down to absorb them rather than the bits they really wanted. Picking up fragments of the noise and converting them into a meaningful message is by and large a random process. 'Hype', that product of the PR industry intended to separate 'desirable objects of attention' from non-productive (read, unprofitable) noise (objects like full-page commercials announcing the premiere of a new film, the launch of a new book, the broadcast of a TV show heavily subscribed to by the advertisers, or the opening of a new exhibition), serves momentarily to divert, channel and condense in a single direction the continuous and desperate, yet scattered search for 'filters'– focusing attention, for a few minutes or a few days, on a selected object of consuming desire.

To quote Eriksen once more: 'Instead of ordering knowledge in tidy rows, information society offers cascades of decontextualized signs more or less randomly connected to each other. . .' Put differently: when growing amounts of information are distributed at a growing speed, it becomes increasingly difficult to create narratives, orders and developmental sequences. The fragments threaten to become hegemonic. This has consequences for the ways we relate to knowledge, work and lifestyle in a wide sense.

Robert Louis Stevenson's memorable verdict, 'to travel hopefully is a better thing than to arrive', has never sounded truer than it does now in our liquidized and fluid modern world. When destinations move, and those that don't lose their charm faster than people can walk, cars drive or planes fly, keeping on the move matters more than the destination. Avoiding making a habit of anything being practised at the moment, or being tied up by the legacy of one's own past, wearing one's current identity like a shirt that can be promptly replaced when it falls out of fashion, scorning past lessons and disdaining past skills without inhibition or regret: these are all becoming the hallmarks of today's liquid modern life politics and attributes of liquid modern rationality. Liquid modern culture no longer feels like a culture of learning and accumulation like the cultures recorded in historians' and ethnographers' reports. Instead it looks like a *culture of disengagement, discontinuity, and forgetting*.

In what George Steiner called 'casino culture', every cultural product is calculated for maximal impact (that is, to break up, push out and dispose of the cultural products of yesterday) and instant obsolescence (that is, to shorten the distance between novelty and rubbish bin, with cultural products wary of outstaying their welcome and quickly vacating the stage to clear the site for the new ones of tomorrow). Artists who once would have identified the value of their work with its eternal duration, and so struggled for a perfection that would render further change all but impossible, now put together installations intended to be pulled apart when the exhibition closes or happenings that will end the moment the actors decide to turn the other way; they wrap up bridges until traffic is restarted or unfinished buildings until the building work is resumed; they erect or carve 'space sculptures' that invite nature to take its toll and supply another proof, if another proof is needed, of the ludicrous brevity of all human deeds and the shallowness of their traces. TV quiz competitors are the only ones who are expected, let alone encouraged, to remember yesterday's talk-of-the-town, though no one is expected, let alone allowed, to opt out of the talk-of-the-town of today.

The consumer market is adapted to the liquid modern 'casino culture', which in turn is adapted to that market's pressures and seductions. The two chime well with each other and feed off each other. In order not to waste their clients' time or pre-empt their future and still unpredictable joys, consumer markets offer products meant for immediate consumption, preferably one-off use with rapid disposal and replacement, so that the living space won't become cluttered once the currently admired and coveted objects fall out of fashion. The clients, confused by the mind-boggling variety of offers and the vertiginous pace at which they change, can no longer rely on a facility to learn and memorize – so they must (and do, gratefully) accept the reassurances that the product currently on offer is '*the* thing', the '*hot* thing', the '*must have*' and the '*must be seen (in or with)* thing'. The hundred-year-old fantasy of Lewis Carroll has now turned into reality: 'it takes all the running *you* can do, to keep in the same place. If you want to get somewhere else, you must run at least twice as fast as that!' So where does this leave the learners and their teachers?

In my youth I kept being warned: 'quickly learned, quickly forgotten'. . . . But it was a different wisdom speaking: a wisdom of a time that held the long term in the highest esteem, when people at the top marked their high position by surrounding themselves with durables and left the transient to those lower down the ladder; that was a time when a capacity for keeping, guarding, caring for and preserving counted for much more than a (regrettable, shaming and bewailed) facility of disposal.

This was not the kind of wisdom many of us would

---

approve of today. What was once merit has nowadays turned into vice. The art of surfing has taken over the top position in the hierarchy of useful and desirable skills from the art of fathoming. If quick forgetting is the consequence of quick and perfunctory learning, long live quick (short, momentary, shallow) learning! After all, if it is tomorrow's commentary on tomorrow's events that you need to compose, the memory of the events of the day before yesterday will be of little help. And since the capacity of memory, unlike the capacity of servers, can't be stretched, a good memory – that is, a long memory – may, if anything, constrain your ability to absorb and speed up assimilation.

Remember that all or almost all contemporary heroes of 'rags-to-riches' stories, guys who made billion-dollar fortunes out of a single felicitous idea and lucky chance, the present-day incarnations of the idea of successful life, from Steve Jobs, founder of Apple, down to Twitter's inventor Jack Dorsey and the founder of Tumblr David Karp – all without exception are education dropouts (with Karp beating the record by spending not a single day on campus after dropping out of high school in his first year). Damien Hirst, another embodiment of instantaneous life success ending in a fabulous fortune, an idol of 'Britart', the most profitable variety of present-day art-making in Britain, confesses his amazement at how much one can achieve with a mediocre grade in school art lessons, a bit of luck and a chainsaw. . .

Haven't we arrived full circle from the myth of the 'rags to riches', the shoeshine boy who turns millionaire just by a stroke of luck combined with rather a lot of gumption, to a 'new and improved' version of the same myth, though with the shoeshining replaced by message kneading? Somewhere along that circular move, the promise to level up chances by universal, life-enhancing education has been lost. . .

8
Minutes to destroy, years to build

Riccardo Mazzeo Among the images that have impressed me and that I have decided to keep there is a photograph of an open air classroom taken in the town of Fada, Chad. Each of the fifty or so primary school children proudly shows a little blackboard over their head; they are poorly dressed, and the country is in trouble because of war, scarce resources and the challenge of 200 different ethnic groups, but all the same there is something 'joyful and glorious' in this picture, as the Italian novelist Antonio Scurati noted: 'the children raising their blackboards look as if they are hoisting the flag of universal schooling, making the cathedral of knowledge culminate in slate pinnacles, the dream of a school building big enough to contain the whole of humankind.'

In Italy, in 1951, the country was underdeveloped and schooling lasted an average of only three years. The country is now 'developed', with an average of eleven years, but this has also depended on the flourishing conditions of the 1960s and the following decades – until recent years, when more and more families are invaded by the spectre of poverty day after day.

In your interview in 2010 with Randeep Ramesh you said of Ed Miliband that you found his vision of community very interesting: his sensibility to the problems of the poor, his awareness that the quality of society and the cohesion of community cannot be estimated in statistical terms but must be gauged in terms of the welfare of the weakest segments of the population. European governments are cutting welfare, in Great Britain, in Italy, almost everywhere. You were perhaps the only one in 1999 who proposed a guarantee on 'citizen's income', essentially, enough money to live a free life, to 'remove the ill-smelling fly of insecurity from the fragrant ointment of freedom'. Ten years on, Ed Miliband has endorsed your proposal, and the young are increasing their awareness of the terrible attacks launched by politicians on their futures, in terms of heavier taxes and greater obstacles. . .

Zygmunt Bauman It takes just a few minutes and a couple of signatures to destroy what took thousands of brains and twice as many hands and lots of years to build. This has always been, perhaps, the most awesome and sinister, yet indomitable attraction of destruction – though the temptation has never been more irresistible than in the hurried lives lived in our speed-obsessed world. In our liquid modern society of consumers, the eviction, removal and disposal industry of riddance is one of the very few businesses assured of continuous growth and immune to the vagaries of consumer markets. That business is, after all, absolutely indispensable for the markets to be able to proceed in the only fashion in which they are capable of acting: stumbling from one round of overshot targets to another, each time clearing away the resulting waste together with the facilities which are blamed for turning it out.

This is obviously an exceedingly wasteful fashion in which to proceed; and indeed, excess and wastefulness are the principal endemic banes of the consumerist economy, pregnant as they are with such a lot of collateral damage and still larger echelons of collateral victims. Excess and waste are the consumerist economy's most loyal, indeed inseparable, fellow travellers – bound to remain inseparable from it until (shared) death do them part. It happens, though, that the timetables of the cycles of excess and waste – normally scattered over the wide spectrum of the consumerist economy and following their own, unsynchronized rhythms – may synchronize, coordinate, overlap and merge, making all but untenable and unattainable any routine patching up of cracks and clefts by the economic equivalents of the cosmetics of face-lifting and skin transplants. When cosmetics won't suffice, full-scale surgery is called for, and – however reluctantly – resorted to. The time of 'retrenchment', 'rearrangement' or 'readjustment' (politically favoured codenames for the slowdown of consumerist activities) and of 'austerity' (the codename for cuts in state expenditure) has arrived, aiming at a 'recovery led by consumers' (the codename for using the cash spared from Treasury coffers to recapitalize consumerism-energizing agencies, mostly banks and issuers of credit cards).

It is in this timespan that we currently live, in the aftermath of the massive accumulation and congestion of excess and waste and the resulting collapse of the credit system, with its countless collateral casualties. In the credit-supported life strategy of 'enjoy now, pay later' – fostered, nourished and boosted by the joint forces of marketing techniques and governmental policies (drilling successive cohorts of students in the art and the habit of living on credit) – consumer markets found a magic wand with which to transform hosts of Cinderellas, inactive or good-for-nothing consumers into a mass of (profit-generating) debtors; even though, as with Cinderella, it was for one ravishing night only. The wand did its magic with the help of assurances that when it came to paying up, the needed cash would be easily drawn out of the accrued market value of the wonders purchased. Prudently left out of the advertising leaflets was the fact that market values go on accruing *because* of the assurance that the ranks of willing and capable buyers of those wonders will keep growing, and so the reasoning behind such assurances is, like all bubbles, circular. If you believed the pushers of credit, you would expect the mortgage loan you took out on your house would be repaid by the house itself, rising in price as it had been through recent years, and bound to go on rising well after the loan was repaid in full. Or you would believe that the loan you took out to finance your university study would be repaid, with huge interest, by the fabulous salaries and perks of office awaiting the holders of diplomas. . .

The bubble has now burst, and the truth did out – though, as usual, *after* the damage was done. And instead of the gains tantalizingly promised to be privatized by the invisible hand of the market, the losses have now been forcibly nationalized by a government bent on promoting consumer liberties and eulogizing consumption as the shortest and surest shortcut to happiness. It is the victims of the excess-and-waste economy who are forced to pay its costs, whether or not they trusted its sustainability and whether or not they believed its promises and willingly surrendered to its temptations. Those who inflated the bubble and gained from it show few if any signs of suffering. *Theirs* are not the houses being repossessed, *their* unemployed benefits are not being cut, *their* children's playgrounds are not the ones ordered to remain unbuilt. It is the people cajoled and forced into dependency on borrowed money who are being punished. As The *Guardian* informed us on 6 February 2011, the government 'would not provide fresh funding for a series of schemes aimed at helping households stay out of debt. Ministers have said there will be no money for the Financial Inclusion Fund, which bankrolled debt advice services, when funding ends this year. The government is also refusing to guarantee the future of the Growth Fund – which dispensed low-interest loans. The Saving Gateway fund, which encouraged those on tax credits and benefits to save, has also been axed.'

Among the millions of those punished, there are hundreds of thousands of youngsters who believed, or were given no choice but to behave *as if* they believed, that the room at the top is boundless, that a university diploma is all you need to be let in, and that once you were there the repayment of the loans you took out along the way would be childishly easy, considering the new credit-worthiness that would come together with that top address. They are now facing the prospect of scribbling innumerable job applications which are hardly ever answered, of infinitely long unemployment, and of the acceptance of wobbly jobs without a future, miles below the top room, as their sole alternative.

It is true that every generation has its measure of outcasts. . . There are people in each generation assigned to outcast status because a 'generational change' is bound to bring some significant changes in life conditions and life demands that will force realities to depart from the expectations implanted by the conditions as they were before and devalue the skills that used to be developed and promoted. These changes will mean that at least some of the new arrivals who are not flexible or prompt enough to adapt to the emergent standards will be ill-prepared to cope with the novel challenges, and ill-equipped to resist their pressures. It does not happen often, however, that the plight of the outcast stretches to embrace a *generation as a whole*. This may be happening now. . .

Several generational changes have been noted in the course of the postwar history of Europe. There was a 'boom generation' first, followed by two generations called respectively X and Y; most recently (though not as recently as the shock of the collapse of Reaganite/ Thatcherite economy), the impending arrival of the Z generation was announced. Each of these generational changes were more or less traumatic events; in each case they signalled a break in continuity and a necessity for sometimes painful readjustments caused by a clash between inherited and learned expectations and unanticipated realities. And yet, looking back from the second decade of the twenty-first century, we can hardly fail to notice that when we are confronted with the profound changes brought about by the latest economic collapse, each of those previous passages between generations may well seem to be the epitome of inter-generational continuity. . .

After several decades of rising expectations, the graduate newcomers to adult life are confronting *falling* expectations – falling much too steeply and abruptly for any hope of a gentle and safe descent. There was bright, dazzling light at the end of every one of the few tunnels their predecessors might have been forced to pass through in the course of their lives; now there is a long, dark tunnel instead, with just a few blinking, flickering and fast fading lights vainly trying to pierce through the gloom.

This is the first post-war generation facing the prospect of downward mobility. Their elders were trained to expect, matter-of-factly, that their children would aim higher and reach further than they themselves had managed to dare and achieve: they expected the inter-generational 'reproduction of success' to go on beating their own records as easily as they themselves used to overtake the achievements of their parents. Generations of parents were used to expecting that their children would have an even wider range of choices, each more attractive than the other; be even better educated, climb even higher in the hierarchy of learning and professional excellence, be richer and feel even more secure. Their own point of arrival, so they believed, would be their children's starting point – and a point with even more roads stretching ahead, all leading upwards.

The youngsters of the generation now entering or preparing to enter the so-called 'labour market' have been groomed and honed to believe that their life task is to outshoot and leave behind their parents' success stories, and that such a task (barring a cruel blow of fate or their own, eminently curable inadequacy) is fully within their capacity. However far their parents have reached, they will reach further. So they, at any rate, have been taught and indoctrinated to believe. Nothing has prepared them for the arrival of the hard, uninviting and inhospitable new world of the downgrading of grades, the devaluation of earned merits, locked doors, the volatility of jobs and the stubbornness of joblessness, the transience of prospects and the durability of defeats; of a new world of stillborn projects and frustrated hopes and of chances ever more conspicuous by their absence.

The last decades were times of the unbounded expansion of every and any form of higher education and of an unstoppable rise in the size of student cohorts. A university degree promised plum jobs, prosperity and glory, a volume of rewards steadily rising to match the steadily expanding ranks of degree holders. With coordination between demand and offer ostensibly preordained, assured and well-nigh automatic, the seductive power of the promise was all but impossible to resist. Now, however, the throngs of the seduced are turning wholesale, and almost overnight, into crowds of the frustrated. For the first time in living memory, the *whole class of graduates* faces a high probability, almost the certainty, of ad hoc, temporary, insecure and part-time jobs, unpaid 'trainee' pseudo-jobs deceitfully rebranded 'practices' – all considerably below the skills they have acquired and eons below the level of their expectations; or of a stretch of unemployment lasting longer than it'll take for the next class of graduates to add their names to the already uncannily long job-centre waiting lists.

In a capitalist society like ours, geared in the first instance to the defence and preservation of prevailing privileges and only as a distant (and much less respected or attended to) second to the lifting of the rest out of their deprivation, this class of graduates, high on goals while being low on means, has no one to turn to for assistance and remedy. People at the helm, whether on the right or the left of the political spectrum, are all up in arms when it comes to protecting their currently muscular constituencies – against the newcomers who are still slow in flexing their laughably immature muscles, and in all probability deferring any real attempt to flex them in earnest until after the next general election. Just as we all, collectively, regardless of the peculiarities of generations, tend to be all too eager to defend our comforts against the demands for livelihood of as yet unborn generations. . .

In noting the 'anger, even hate' that can be observed in the 2010 class of graduates, political scientist Louis Chavel, in his article published in *Le Monde* on 4 January 2011 under the title 'Les jeunes sont mal partis', asks how long it will be before the rancour of the French contingent of baby-boomers infuriated by the threats to their pension nests combines with that of the class of 2010 denied the exercise of their right to earn a pension. But combine into what, we may (and should) ask? Into a new war of generations? Into a new leap into the pugnacity of the extremist fringes surrounding an increasingly despondent and dejected middle? Or into a supragenerational consent that this world of ours, notable as it is for using duplicity as its survival weapon and for burying hopes alive, is no longer sustainable and in need of an already grossly delayed refurbishment?

But what about the graduates yet to come? And what about the society in which they will have to take over, sooner rather than later, the tasks their elders were assumed to perform and for better or worse did? That society in which they will determine sum total of skills, – whether they like it or not, and whether by design or by default – the knowledge, competitiveness, stamina and guts, along with its ability to face challenges, to get the better of them and self-improve.

It would be premature and irresponsible to speak of the planet as a whole entering the postindustrial era. But it would be no less irresponsible to deny that Great Britain entered such an era quite a few decades ago. Through the twentieth century, British industry shared the lot suffered by British agriculture in the nineteenth century – it started the century overcrowded, and left it depopulated (in fact, in all the 'most developed' Western countries, industrial workers currently constitute less than 18 per cent of working population). What has been all too often overlooked, however, is that in parallel with the numbers of industrial workers among the national labour force, the ranks of industrialists among the elite of wealth and political power also shrank. We continue to live in a capitalist society, but the capitalists who set the tune and pay the pipers are no longer owners of mines, docks or steel and automobile plants. On the list of the richest 1 per cent of Americans, only one in six names belongs to an industrial entrepreneur; the rest are financiers, lawyers, doctors, scientists, architects, programmers, designers, and all sorts of stage, screen and stadium celebrities. The biggest money is now to be found in the handling and allocation of finances and in the invention of new technical gadgets, utensils of communication, and marketing and publicity gimmicks, as well as in the arts and entertainment universe;

in other words, in new, as yet unexploited, imaginative and catching ideas. It is people with brilliant and useful (read, sellable) ideas that nowadays inhabit the rooms at the top. It is these people who contribute most to what is currently understood as 'economic growth'. The primary 'deficit resources' from which capital is made and whose possession and management provides the primary source of wealth and power are nowadays, in the postindustrial era, knowledge, inventiveness, imagination, the ability to think and the courage to think differently – qualities that universities were called on to create, disseminate and instil.

About a hundred years ago, at the time of the Boer War, panic struck people concerned with the might and prosperity of the nation at the news of large and growing numbers of undernourished recruits, decrepit in body and in poor health, and for that reason physically and mentally unfit for factory floors and battlefields. Now is the time for panic at the prospect that there will be rising numbers of people who are undereducated (certainly undereducated by the world's fast-rising standards) and so unfit for research laboratories, designer workshops, lecture theatres, artists' studios or information networks, as a result of the shrinking of university resources and the falling numbers of high-class university graduates. Governments' cuts in higher education funding manage to be, at the same time, cuts in the life prospects of the generation coming of age and in the future standard and standing of British civilization, as well as in Britain's European and world status and role.

Cuts in the government funding come together with the unprecedentedly steep, indeed savage rises in university fees. We are used to feeling alarmed by, and fulminating against, a few per cent rise in the cost of train tickets, beef, electricity; we tend to be aghast and baffled, however, when faced by a rise of 300 per cent, feeling incapacitated and disarmed, not really knowing how to react. . . In the arsenal of our defensive weapons, there are none we can resort to – just as happened in the recent case of those billions and trillions of dollars, pumped in one go by governments into the strong rooms of banks after dozens of years of penny-pinching and subsequent litigation about a few millions that had been deducted or should have been added to the budgets of schools, hospitals, welfare funds or urban renewal projects. We can hardly imagine the misery and anguish of our grandchildren as they awaken to their inheritance of a hitherto unimaginable volume of national debt clamouring for repayment; we are still not ready to visualize it, even now, when courtesy of our own government we have been offered the chance of tasting the first sample spoonful of the bitter brew which they, our grandchildren, will be force-fed by the cauldronful. And we can hardly imagine as yet the full reach of the social and cultural devastation that is bound to follow the erection of a monetary version of the walls of Berlin or Palestine at the entry to the knowledge distribution centres. Yet we must, and we should – at our shared future peril.

Talents, insightfulness, inventiveness, adventurousness – all those rough stones waiting to be polished into diamonds by talented, insightful, inventive and adventurous teachers inside university buildings – are spread more or less evenly through the human species, even if we are prevented from perceiving it by artificial barriers erected by humans on the path of human beings from *zoon*, 'bare life', to *bios*, social life. Rough diamonds do not select the lodes in which nature has cast them and care little about divisions invented by humans; though those divisions invented by humans take care to select some of them into a class earmarked for polishing, and to relegate others to the might-have-been category – as well as doing all they can to cover up the traces of that operation. The tripling of fees will inevitably decimate the rank of youngsters who are growing up in the mean districts of social and cultural deprivation and yet are determined and daring enough to knock on the university doors of opportunity – and so will deprive the rest of the nation of the share of rough diamonds youngsters like these used to contribute year after year. And as life success, and particularly upward social mobility, nowadays tends to be enabled, prompted and set in motion by the meeting of knowledge with talent, insightfulness, inventiveness and spirit of adventure, the tripling of fees will pull British society at least half a century back in its drive towards classlessness. Just a few decades after being flooded with scholarly discoveries of a 'farewell to class', we can expect, in the not so distant future, a spate of treatises on 'welcome back, class – all is forgotten'.

Expect it indeed we may – and, therefore, being the socially responsible creatures we academics need and are expected to be, we should worry about a kind of damage even more damaging than the immediate effects of throwing universities at the mercy of consumer markets (which is what the combination of the state retreating from its patronage and a tripling of fees amounts to), in terms of redundancies and the suspension or abandonment of research projects and probably also a further worsening of staff/student ratios, and so also of teaching conditions and quality. And expect indeed the resurrection of class divisions, because more than enough reasons have been created for less well-off parents to think twice before committing their children to more debts in three years than they themselves incurred over their lifetime; and for the children of those parents, watching their slightly older acquaintances lining up in front of job agencies, to think twice about the sense of it all – of committing themselves to three years of drudgery and life in poverty only to confront a set of options at the end not much more prepossessing than the ones they currently face. . .

Well, it takes just a few minutes and a couple of signatures to destroy what took thousands of brains and twice as many hands and lots of years to build.

9

The young as a tip for the consumer industry

Riccardo Mazzeo In our 'world of consumers', in addition to the young who, although in a milder way than their Tunisian or Egyptian peers, rightly rebel against an unfair power, there are many youngsters who don't respect adults at all, who have lost a sense of the principle noted by Miguel Benasayag and Gerard Schmit in their book on 'the era of the sad passions': 'priority/authority', that is, the right of a parent or teacher who has lived in this world for a longer time to be respected by children.[8] More than sixty years ago Adorno described such an unexpected attitude in the second aphorism of *Minima Moralia*:

> In the antagonistic society even the relationship between generations is a relationship of competition, behind which the plain, unvarnished violence is hidden. But today we are beginning to slide back towards a stage that does not know the Oedipus complex, but rather parricide. The elimina-

8   M. Benasayag and G. Schmit, *Les passions tristes. Souffrance psychique et crise sociale* (Paris: La Découverte, 2003).

tion of very old people is one of the symbolic misdeeds of Nazism. . . . We must notice with terror that often, setting ourselves against our parents as representatives of the world, we already were, unawares, the spokespersons of an even worse world.[9]

The phenomenon of 'paedophobia' is more and more widespread and more than half of parents are afraid of being physically abused by their adolescent sons.

Zygmunt Bauman 'Increasingly viewed as yet another social burden, youth are no longer included in a discourse about the promise of a better future. Instead they are now considered part of a disposable population whose presence threatens to recall repressed collective memories of adult responsibility' – so writes Henry A. Giroux in an essay of 3 February 2011 titled 'Youth in the Era of Disposability'.[10]

As a matter of fact, the young are not fully, unambiguously disposable. What salvages them from straightforward disposability – if only just – and secures a measure of adult attention is their current and still more their potential contribution to consumer demand. Successive echelons of youth mean a perpetual supply of unspoilt 'virgin land' ready for cultivation, without which even the simple reproduction of the capitalist economy, not to mention economic growth, would be all but inconceivable. Young people are thought of and paid attention to as 'yet another market'

9 T.W. Adorno, *Minima Moralia: Reflections from Damaged Life* (London: New Left Books, 1974).
10 See http://bad.eserver.org/issues/2011/Giroux-Youth.html (accessed Oct. 2011).

to be commodified and exploited. Giroux continues: 'Through the educational force of a culture that commercializes every aspect of kids' lives, using the Internet and various social networks along with the new media technologies such as cell phones', corporate institutions aim at 'immersing young people in the world of mass consumption in ways more direct and expansive than anything we have seen in the past.' A recent study by the Kaiser Family Foundation found that 'young people aged eight to eighteen now spend more than seven and a half hours a day with smart phones, computers, televisions, and other electronic devices, compared with less than six and a half hours five years ago. When you add the additional time youth spend texting, talking on their cell-phones or doing multiple tasks, such as "watching TV while updating Facebook" – the number rises to eleven hours of total media content each day.'

One can go on adding ever new evidence to that collected by Giroux; a gathering volume of evidence casting 'the problem of youth' fairly and squarely as an issue of 'drilling them into consumers', and leaving all other youth-related issues on a side shelf, or effacing them altogether from the political, social and cultural agenda. On the one hand, as I have already noted, severe limitations imposed on governmental funding of higher education coupled with equally savage rises in university fees – indeed, the state deciding to wash its hands of its obligation to 'educate people', blatantly so in the case of its 'cutting edge', bridgehead or frontline areas, but somewhat more obliquely, as in the idea of replacing state-run secondary schools with 'academies' run by the consumer market, also at the levels destined to determine the overall volume of knowledge and skills at the nation's disposal as well as its distribution among categories of population – testify to a fading of interest in youth as the future political and cultural elite of the nation. On the other hand, quite new vistas are opened by Facebook, for instance, but other 'social websites' too, for agencies bent on focusing on youth and tackling them primarily as 'virgin land' waiting to be conquered and exploited by the advancing consumerist troops.

Thanks to the happy-go-lucky and enthusiastic self-exposure of Facebook addicts to thousands of online friends and millions of online flâneurs, marketing managers can harness the most intimate and ostensibly the most 'personal' and 'unique', articulated or half-conscious, already boiling or only projected desires and wants to the consumerist juggernaut, what will pop up on Facebook-fed screens will now be a *personal* offer, prepared, groomed and caringly honed 'especially for you' – an offer you can't refuse because you are unable to resist its temptation; after all, it is what you fully and truly needed all the time it 'fits your unique personality' and 'makes a statement' to that effect, the statement you always wanted to make, showing you to be that one and only unique personality that you are. This is a genuine breakthrough, if there ever was one, in the fortunes of marketing.

It is well known that the lion's share of the money spent on marketing is consumed by the exorbitantly costly effort to detect, instil and cultivate in the prospective shopper desires that can be reforged into a decision to obtain the particular product on offer. A certain Sal Abdin, a marketing adviser active on the web, says as much about the task to be confronted when he addresses the following counsel to the adepts of the marketing art:

if you sell drills, write an article on how to make better holes, and you'll get lots more sales leads than merely advertising information about your drills and drill specifications. Why does that work? Because nobody who bought a drill wanted a drill. They wanted a hole. Offer information about making holes and you'll be much more successful. If you're selling a course on losing weight, sell the benefits of being slim, of being more healthy, of feeling better, the fun of shopping for clothes, how the opposite sex will respond. . . know what I mean? Sell the benefits of the product and the product will sell itself when buyers reach the sales page. Mention its features but really emphasize what it can do for the buyer to make life better, easier, faster, happier, more successful. . . get my drift?[11]

This is not the promise of an easy life, to be sure. Nor of a short, smooth and fast road to the target, which is the meeting of a customer wanting to buy and a product wanting to be sold. Developing a desire for beautiful holes, and linking it to a drill that promises to make them, is not perhaps an impossible task, but it will take time and skill to make it settle in the reader's imagination and lift it close to the top of the reader's dreams. The wished-for encounter will eventually happen, but the road leading to that glorious moment of fulfilment is long, rough and bumpy and, above all, there is no guarantee you will reach the destination until you've got there. And in addition, that road needs to be well paved and wide enough to accommodate an unknown number of walkers – but in all probability, the number of people actually deciding to walk it won't justify the huge

11 See http://salabdin.com/w/?p=103 (accessed Oct. 2011).

expenditure needed to make it so broad, pleasurable to walk on, tempting and inviting.

This is precisely why I called the opportunity presented by Facebook 'a genuine breakthrough'. It is an opportunity to do nothing less than cut out the costs of road-building from the marketing budget altogether – or almost. As in the case of so many other responsibilities, it shifts the task of developing desires in prospective clients from the (marketing) managers to the clients themselves. Thanks to the databank volunteered by Facebook users (unpaid!), and expanded daily, marketing offers can now unfailingly spot customers who are already 'prepared', mellowed and matured, complete with the right kinds of desires (and therefore hardly needing to be lectured on the beauty of holes) – they can reach them directly while donning the doubly attractive disguise, flattering in addition to being welcome, of a blessing that is 'your own, made especially for you, to meet your own, personal needs'.

Just an inane question for our inane times: is the last barrier standing between youth and its disposal perhaps its newly discovered and enabled capacity to serve as a disposal tip for the excesses of the consumer industry in our era of disposability?

10

The effort to improve mutual understanding is a prolific source of human creativity

Riccardo Mazzeo I've just read your interview with the Italian monthly magazine *E*, where you say that the Turks who live in Germany 'love their new country, want to live in the German system, but only "contemplate" becoming German', and I couldn't help recalling an article a month ago by the Berlin correspondent of *Corriere della Sera* who told the following story. A group of German families began screaming when they saw the barbecue of a Turkish family on the grass, and obliged them to put it out immediately, disgusted by the smell of their food. Then they set up camp five metres away and stripped naked to enjoy the sun, as autochthons normally do. You can imagine the Turkish father's anger and the bafflement of the Turkish mother and daughter at this offence to their modesty. In his most recent book, *La vie en double: Ethnologie, voyage et écriture*, Marc Augé describes it as the task of anthropology to be able to tackle not only extra-

European populations but also 'the slippery complexity of the Western world'. Even what seems 'natural' is indeed a cultural construction and varies in different contexts, eras and traditions. This kind of thinking is subversive because it denies the existence of absolute truths, and consequently the legitimacy of every form of power. Augé compares the anthropologist to the hero of the famous Stendhal novel *La chartreuse de Parme*, Fabrizio Del Dongo, who in the middle of the Battle of Waterloo cannot manage to understand what's going on. The same thing happens to the anthropologist who has limited vision and cannot grasp the whole planetary battle, and this is especially true for the heads of government of the United Kingdom and Germany, David Cameron and Angela Merkel, who announce the death of multiculturalism from the very narrow perspective of their reluctance to explore and give a chance to ways of coexistence different from the no longer applicable model of assimilation.

I think that the slow process towards a new and respectful way of coexisting cannot come from our politicians, who, as you admirably explained in your earlier answers, are too focused on maintaining their privileges; it has to come from the simmering and bubbling laboratory of interrelations between youngsters.

Zygmunt Bauman The art of passing information from one culture to another is something about which anthropologists have thought long and hard; without so far finding a risk-free, flawless, patented method. At the most, they have arrived at recipes for how to proceed, but not at foolproof guarantees of arrival. A complete 'fusion of horizons', which in Hans Gadamer's view is the condition sine qua non of unerring understanding, is a distant prospect, perhaps an unreachable target. The practice of intercultural communication is full of traps, and misapprehensions are the rule rather than the exception, because no pair of cultural idioms fully translates one to the other: if a message is to be fully understood by the recipient, it needs to be somewhat adjusted to the recipient's frame of mind and therefore distorted; if it is to retain its pristine form, it will have to brace itself for being only partly comprehended. This, at any rate, is the state of the game so far – undoubtedly a nuisance, though not in my view a tragedy, because we have managed somehow, despite everything, to communicate cross-culturally; and more importantly still, because the strenuous effort to improve mutual understanding has proved to be, although (or rather thanks to) being doomed, a prolific source of cultural creativity.

Of the many varieties of advice on 'how to proceed', let me name Norbert Elias's conception of 'engagement and detachment', suggesting that the effort of mutual understanding needs to manoeuvre between the extremes of complete identification with the Other and complete separation from them, always staying wary of coming too close to one extreme or the other. Or another stratagem, of 'surrender and catch', promoted by Kurt Wolff: insert yourself as deep as possible into another culture, penetrate whatever it has that is unique, and bring the rich spoils home. . . Both recipes, much like Bronisław Malinowski's 'participant observation', start and proceed, however, from the premise of a strict division between researcher and researched, subject and object in the intercultural encounter: I, the anthropologist, intend to acquire knowledge of how the other

Mutual understanding as a source of creativity

side lives – while remaining oblivious to the presence or absence of progress in that other side's comprehension of how I, and people at my home, live. . . The big question is, of course, whether such one-directional instructions are of any use in cases other than a single anthropologist's one-off visit to an exotic land; whether they can serve the needs of permanent cohabitation and cooperation between different cultures.

To answer that question, even if in a preliminary fashion, let me refer you to the experience of Frank Cushing, a genuine pioneer of the practice of 'participant observation' *avant la lettre*, thirty years before Malinowski's exile to the Trobriand Isles (Malinowski, a citizen of Austro-Hungary, was caught in Australia by the outbreak of the Great War and promptly deported as an enemy alien far from Australian shores). Cushing lived the years 1879–84 among Indians of the Zuni tribe. A keen, dedicated and conscientious anthropologist, he did his best to try to penetrate deeper and deeper into the Zuni *Lebenswelt*, but was continuously frustrated (indeed, to the point of despair) by the feeling that whenever he tried to convey his findings to anthropologists in a form they were able to grasp, he was doing an injustice to the meanings invested by Zuni. Cushing went further than any anthropologist before him, and than most after him, to 'participate' in the natives' form of life. He ended up being accepted by the Zuni as 'one of their own' – an unheard-of attainment confirmed by his promotion to the priesthood or Rainbow, the supreme object of the Zunis' cult. After that, however, the story goes, he had nothing to tell his fellow anthropologists. As 'one of the Zunis', he had turned from the subject into an object of anthropological inquiry. . . Cushing dedicated the rest of his life to promoting of the idea of 'reciprocal anthropology', implying two-directionality in the encounter and mutuality in the study; ultimately, an equality of the sides in a simultaneously learning and teaching situation, each side exploring the other while being explored. This, I guess, is what is truly relevant to the context in which we, lay people, become conscious of misunderstandings in our daily lives, become aware that communication between cultures (including generation-bound cultures) creates a 'problem' yearning to be 'resolved', and crave a way out of the quandary.

So we are back to Gadamer. And to his verdict that the ultimate target of the 'fusion of horizons' is as desirable and worth pursuing as it is unlikely, and perhaps impossible, to be reached.

II

The unemployed can always play lotto, can't they?

Riccardo Mazzeo Around the end of last year, your colleague Anthony Giddens criticized the rise in tuition fees, saying that such a decision was going to change the university into a supermarket, and that it was not only ethically unfair but also economically counterproductive because impeding smart but poor students from attending university would mean inconceivable losses for the whole society. Your analysis of this phenomenon is more radical and comprehensive, so it would be useless to compare your two visions of the problem. There is only one aspect of his subject that I would like to put under your scrutiny: he says that the fact of being heavily indebted to the state will orient students towards faculties that guarantee large profits after their degree, and most of them will try to become managers, bankers, lawyers and engineers, to the detriment of classical studies.

In her book *Not for Profit: Why Democracy Needs the Humanities*, Martha Nussbaum vigorously upholds liberal education, comparing particularly the educational systems of the United States and India, and Tullio De Mauro, in his introduction to the Italian edition of the book, underlines the complexity of what we tend to call either 'school' or 'education'. So, while in the United States a simplified, mechanical vision of the relationship between school and economic development prevails (in a quotation from Robert J. Samuelson in *Newsweek*: 'Americans have an extravagant faith in the ability of education to solve all manner of social problems'), with students regularly choosing hard sciences, and Austria, Denmark, France, Germany, the United Kingdom, Belgium, Ireland and Portugal are more and more affected by a contraction of classical studies, in other countries the relationship with the humanities is alive and flourishing. In India, the classical foundation of education has given birth to great mathematicians and economists; in China the classical texts are systematically studied; in Japan, Chinese ideogram learning (their Greek) is compulsory; in Israel biblical Hebrew has been the starting point for the birth and the spread of neo-Hebrew.

I think that pursuing merely technical or scientific learning, forgetting the wider and richer critical horizon uniquely offered by classical, historical and philosophical education, is (in De Mauro's words) 'incomplete and fruitless', just as it is sterile and dangerous to believe you can master the entire world thanks to the internet when you do not have the culture that would permit you to find and sift good information from bad.

Zygmunt Bauman The most prestigious academic institutions issuing the most prestigious academic diplomas – institutions that have been generous in granting social privileges or making up for social deprivation – are year by year, one step at a time, yet consistently and relentlessly, drifting out of the 'social' market and distancing themselves ever further from the throngs of youngsters whose hopes of glittering prizes they kindled and inflamed. As William D. Cohan tells us in the *New York Times* of 16 March 2011, the annual price of tuition and other fees at Harvard University have risen by 5 per cent every year over the last twenty years. This year, the price has reached $52,000. 'Generally speaking, in order to pay just Harvard's tuition, someone would have to earn more than $100,000 in annual pretax compensation. And there are all the other family expenses – among them, the gasoline, the mortgage, food and medical expenses. . . Very quickly the numbers get astronomical.'

And yet. . . Of 30,000 applicants to Harvard last year, only 7.2 per cent were admitted. Demand for places has been – still is – high. There are still thousands of parental couples for whom the tuition fees, however exorbitant, are not an obstacle, and it is just a routine matter for their children to go to Harvard or another elite academic establishment – the exercise of an inherited right and fulfilment of a family duty, the last finishing touch before settling into one's legitimate place inside the country's wealth elite. Though there are still thousands more parental couples ready for whatever financial sacrifice is required to help their children to join that elite, thereby making their grandchildren's place in the elite a legitimate expectation. For the latter, painfully wounded in their parental ambitions and their trust in the American Dream when the universities turned away from their imputed or claimed role of promoters of social mobility, Cohan has words of consolation: he suggests that perhaps 'the best and brightest among us will always find a way to achieve their inevitable level of excellence, *with or without the benefit of a traditional education*' (italics added). To make that promise sound plausible and believable, he adds a list of the impressive and fast-growing numbers of new billionaires who are all, without exception, education dropouts. Well, with secure industrial employment no longer on offer, the unemployed can always play lotto, can't they?

A high-class diploma from a high-class university was for many years the best investment that loving parents could make for their children and their children's future. Or, at least, so it was believed. That belief, like so many other beliefs that combined into the American (and not just the American) dream of gates opened wide to all hard-working people determined to push them open and keep them open, is now being shattered. The labour market for holders of higher education credentials is currently shrinking – perhaps even faster than the market for those who lack university certificates to enhance their market value. Nowadays, it is not only people who failed to make the right kind of effort and the right kind of sacrifice who find the gates – *expectedly* – shut in their face; people who did everything they believed to be necessary for success are finding themselves – though, in their case, *unexpectedly* – in much the same predicament, turned away from the gates empty-handed. This, to be sure, is an entirely new ball game, as the Americans say. . .

Social promotion through education served for many years as a fig leaf for the naked and indecent inequality of human conditions and prospects: as long as academic achievements correlated with handsome social rewards, people who failed to climb the social ladder had only themselves to blame – and only themselves as the target for their bitterness and wrath. After all (so the educational promise suggested), the better places were reserved for the people who worked better, and good fortune came to people who forced it to be good by diligent learning and the sweat of their brow; if bad fortune was your lot, your learning and your work were obviously not as good as they should have been. That apology for persistent and growing inequality nowadays sounds all but hollow; even more hollow than it would have sounded without the loud proclamations of the advent of the 'knowledge society', a kind of society in which knowledge becomes the prime source of national and personal wealth, and in which the possessors and users of knowledge are accordingly entitled to the lion's share of that wealth.

The shock of the new and rapidly growing phenomenon of graduate unemployment, or graduate employment much below graduate expectations (proclaimed to be legitimate), is a painful blow not just to the minority of zealous climbers, but also to the much wider category of people who meekly suffered their unappetizing lot, numbed by the shame of missing the chances waiting in abundance for those less work-shy than themselves. It is difficult to say whether the effects on the first or the second category will cause more social damage, but together, appearing simultaneously, they make quite an explosive mixture. . . You can almost picture quite a few people at the helm shuddering when they read Cohan's sombre warning and premonition: 'One lesson to be learned from the recent uprising in the

Middle East, especially in Egypt, is that a long-suffering group of highly educated but underemployed people can be the catalyst for long overdue societal change.'

You think this is just one more American idiosyncrasy? You well may think so, because one of the most conspicuous features of the 'American dream' is the belief that things can occur in the United States that in more mundane lands are more or less unimaginable. To pre-empt such a misconception, let's jump a few thousand miles to the east of Eden: to Poland, a country that in the last two decades has experienced an exorbitant rise in the number of higher education establishments, and in their students and graduates, but also in the costs of education – alongside a similarly spectacular rise in income polarization and overall social inequality. What follows is a handful of samples from an extraordinary number of similar cases, as reported on 19 March 2011 by the leading Polish daily, *Gazeta Wyborcza*.[12]

Two years ago Agnieszka graduated with a degree in finance and banking. Her countless job applications remained unanswered. After more than a year of vain efforts and deepening despair, a friend fixed her up with a receptionist job. Among her not especially exciting duties is to collect day in, day out, the CVs of other graduates which are destined to remain, like hers, unanswered. Tomek, graduate of another prestigious college, did not have Agnieszka's luck and had to settle for the job of an estate guard for the equivalent of £280 a month. His colleague from the same graduation ceremony is determined to take any job if, in a few

---

12   At   http://wyborcza.pl/1,75478,9282979,Wyksztalcona_klasa_robotni cza.html#ixzz1H2jStWf4 (accessed Oct. 2011).

more months, nothing remotely related to his acquired and certified skills comes his way. All in all, more and more graduates are putting their university diplomas aside among the family memorabilia and settling for jobs not demanding much skill, as couriers, shop assistants, taxi drivers, waiters (the latter, promising to fatten thin wages with customers' tips, becoming the most popular).

In a report under the title 'Pas de rentrée pour les "Ni-Nis"', *Le Monde* tells the story of seventeen-year-old Yetzel Decerra, who lives with his parents in the north of Mexico and is one of the activists in the Movement of the Excluded from Higher Education, founded in 2006.[13] 'No place for me in public education, no money to study in a private college, and no job', Decerra recites about his plight and that of his hundreds of thousand companions in misery. State-run universities are of a very high standard, yet they are few and far between (of 122,750 applicants to the National Autonomous University of Mexico this year, only 10,300 were offered a place; on a national scale, only one in three candidates can count on admission). Of 28 million Mexicans between fifteen and twenty-nine years of age, 19 million don't attend any educational institution, while 7.5 million are looking in vain for jobs. Decerra's Movement of the Excluded is fighting for university places for 200,000 impecunious youngsters who are eager to study.

From Hudson to Vistula through Mexico City, there are similar sights and sounds; the same deafening clatter of gates being shut and locked, the same off-putting picture of rapidly rising heaps of frustrated hopes. In

13 *Le Monde*, 28 August 2011.

our societies with allegedly knowledge-powered and information-driven economies and education-driven economic success, knowledge seems to be failing to guarantee success, and education failing to deliver that knowledge. The vision of education-driven upward mobility, neutralizing the toxins of inequality, making them liveable with and rendering them harmless, and yet more disastrously the vision of education being able to keep upward social mobility in operation – these two visions are beginning simultaneously to evaporate. Their dissipation spells trouble for education as we know it. But it also spells trouble for the excuse favoured and commonly used in our society in the effort to justify its injustices.

Milan Kundera memorably observed that the uni-fication of humanity has thus far consisted in having nowhere to escape. How true. Perhaps for no one more true than for the young, that sole foothold of humanity in the land of the future. . . At any rate, some French observers are hastening to announce the arrival of the 'Ni-Ni' (not in employment, not in education) generation – perhaps the first truly global generation.

Xavier Decros, the French education minister between 2007 and 2009, announced a great educational reform, promising 'new freedom to families' and favouring 'equality of chances' as well as improving (enhancing) the 'social diversity in colleges and lycées'.[14] A few years later, it was found by two general inspectors of schools that in better–off educational establishments there were few pupils of modest means, whereas students from priv-ileged categories had disappeared. The 'social mixing' of

14 'Bilan scolaire globalement negatif', *Le Monde*, 6 September 2011.

schoolchildren is everywhere in retreat, as a joint result of the *embourgeoisement* of 'well feathered' schools and the proletarianization of the common ones. And it was the same with all the rest of the reform's declared objectives. Having analysed the whole programme of educational reform point by point, the author of the summary, Pierre Merle, Professor of Sociology at the University of Brittany, concluded that the words used in the titles of the successive chapters of the programme (equality of opportunity, social mix, defeat of illiteracy, assistance to children with learning difficulties, rectification of educational priorities) had been misused. The results were the exact opposites of the declared intentions. Clearly, they could not be squared with the logic of the market, which was expected to operate the reform. . .

I2

Disability, abnormality, minority as a political problem

Riccardo Mazzeo   Martha Nussbaum was one of the first philosophers to voice the ethical value of assigning full dignity to disabled people. Dario Ianes has been the scholar in Italy who more than anybody else has contributed with his teaching, books and other activities (he was member of the Italian ministerial commission for school inclusion, but not under Berlusconi's government) to helping people with disabilities or special needs. One of his thirty books, *La Speciale Normalità* (A Special Normality) has been translated abroad, into German and Portuguese, and I would like to quote a passage from this text:

> *I want to do the same things as everybody else.* Only a disabled student could express in one sentence, in a crystal clear formula, the manifold meaning of normality. I want to do the same things as everybody else first of all because I have the same rights. I want to do the same as everybody else because this is a deeply felt need. To be able to do the same things as everybody else is a right, but also a way to

foster social development – I want to do the same things as you do also for your own sake, for you, to help the growth and cohesion of our group.

Thus, normality means equal worth. Normality means first of all *equality of rights* – normality as the equal worth of each one, and as equal rights independently of personal and social conditions. The equal worth of every individual is the foundation of the Italian law, starting with the Constitution. Our legislation recognizes the equal worth, rights, and opportunities of all citizens, and is committed to removing all the obstacles preventing the individual's self-realization.

Even neglecting the fact that such prominent and extremely smart people as Robert J. Sternberg (the past president of the American Psychological Association) or Massimo Recalcati (the most important Italian follower of Jacques Lacan, who has developed theory from many stirring ideas and, unlike Lacan, is capable of making his works intelligible) used to be considered 'retarded children' at primary school, and would have probably been lost forever without the sensitive help of extraordinary teachers, what do you think of the inclusion in school of people in difficulty?

Zygmunt Bauman 'Normality' is an ideologically processed name for the majority. What else does being 'normal' mean, other than falling into a statistical majority? And what else does 'abnormality' mean, if not belonging to a statistical minority? I speak of majorities and minorities, because the idea of normality presumes that some units in an aggregate do not meet the 'norm'; if 100 per cent of units all carried the same traits, the idea of a 'norm' would hardly emerge. So the idea of 'norm' and 'normality' presumes un-sameness: a split of the aggregate into a majority and a minority, into 'most of' and 'some'. The 'ideological processing' I mentioned refers to a superimposing of the 'ought' upon the 'is': not only are units of a certain kind in a majority, but they are as they 'should be', 'right and proper'; conversely, those who lack the attribute in question are what they 'should not be', 'wrong and improper'. The passage from a 'statistical majority' (a statement of fact) to 'normality' (an evaluative judgement), and from a 'statistical minority' to 'abnormality' imputes a difference in quality to the difference in numbers: being in the minority also means inferiority. When a difference in quality is superimposed upon the difference in numbers and applied to interhuman relations, the differences in numerical strength are recycled into the phenomenon (both presumed and practised) of *social inequality*. The issue of 'normality versus abnormality' is the form in which the issue of 'majority versus minority' is absorbed and domesticated, and subsequently tackled, in the building and preservation of *social order*. I suspect therefore that 'disability' and 'invalidity', the affiliated names for 'abnormality' (a bit more, though not wholly, 'politically correct'), used when referring to the treatment of human minorities as inferior, are part and parcel of the wider issue of 'majority versus minority' – and so ultimately a *political* problem. That problem focuses on the defence of minority rights, which the current democratic mechanisms, based as they are on merging being in a *majority* with the right to take decisions binding on *all*, seem to be unable (and probably not particularly eager) to confront, handle and definitely resolve.

Disability, abnormality, minority as a political problem

In H. G. Wells's famous story 'The Valley of the Blind', the question is posited and skilfully explored: in a society of the blind, would the one-eyed man be king? That was what was expected by the person who wandered into the valley to escape the society of the two-eyed, where having only one eye was viewed as a demeaning flaw. Were he indeed to become king once in the company of the blind, the tacit assumption underlying our society – that the superiority of seeing over blindness is a verdict of nature, rather than a socio-cultural creation – would be endorsed, reinforced, perhaps 'proved'. But it was not to happen. The one-eyed stranger was not acclaimed as the king to be adored and obeyed, but cast as a monster to be abhorred and chased away! In the 'normality' made to the measure of the inhabitants of the valley, who happened to be blind, he – the one-eyed man – carried a threatening abnormality. Which shows that abnormality does not feel repellent and menacing because of its inherent inferiority, but because of its clash with the order built to suit the needs, habits and expectations of the 'normal' – that is, the majority. All in all, discriminating against the 'abnormal' (to wit, the minority condition) is an activity intended to defend and to preserve order, a socio-cultural creation. . .

In his two-volume story, *Blindness* and *Seeing*, José Saramago developed this topic still further. In the first volume, an inexplicable blindness afflicts the whole population of the city except one woman. On this one-person minority the horrors of the new 'norm' suspending and invalidating all the rules of the old order are focused and magnified in the terrified minds of the blind majority to the status of a major, perhaps even the principal, cause of their miseries. In the second volume, the city has fully recovered from the plague of blindness, but it is afflicted by an equally inexplicable disaster for order: the electorate's unwillingness to go the polls, and so join in with the game of democracy, the currently binding model of order. All the forces of the secret police are then mobilized to hunt for, find and disempower that one woman who in times of blindness failed to lose her powers of sight. Once abnormal, forever abnormal; abnormal in one respect, abnormal in all; and not a threat to one particular order, but to order as such. It is, in the end, all about order.

Order is made to the measure of majority, so that those who are relatively few and unwilling to obey it are in a minority, easy to play down as a 'fringe deviation' – and so easy to spot, locate, disarm and overpower. Selecting, marking and setting aside the 'fringe of abnormality' is a necessary concomitant of order building and the unavoidable cost of an order's perpetuation.

This is an unsavoury, painful and unpalatable truth, yet truth nevertheless. The inhabited world is structured to make it hospitable – convenient and comfortable – for its 'normal' inhabitants: people in the majority. Cars are required to be equipped with lights and horns to warn of their approach – gadgets of no use to those who are blind and deaf. Staircases, intended to facilitate the approach to raised places, are of no help to people confined to wheelchairs. At my advanced age, I have myself lost much of my hearing so I am no longer alerted by the ringing of phones or doorbells. All the examples so far have been connected to bodily impairments, which in a caring society can either be removed by medical means, or mitigated in their absence by technological implements that 'extend' the human body and/or deputize for the missing bodily faculties. There are other kinds of disabilities, however – much more widespread, even though in their case their disabilitating powers are swept under the carpet, hypocritically denied or otherwise argued away and covered up. They are neither medical nor technological problems – but political issues. For instance, handicaps caused to people without cars by cancelling bus routes that are 'unprofitable' (and so uncomfortable for the 'normal' taxpayer) or closing down 'unprofitable' post offices or branches of banks. Particularly in our society of consumers, there are 'disqualified' consumers, short of money, denied credit, and therefore denied the chance of meeting the standards of 'normality' set by the market and measured by the number of possessions and purchasing acts. And most prominently for our theme, there are huge numbers of bodily fit youngsters of school age, disabled in their attempts to reach the standards set by the labour market by the circumstance of being born and growing up in families with below-average earnings or in deprived and neglected neighbourhoods. Families living in poverty (again a condition measured by socio-culturally set standards of 'normality') are the most profuse suppliers of 'educationally substandard' students. In their case political equivalents of the medical or technological ways of compensating for bodily disabilities are called for. These means do exist, but their availability or absence depends only in a relatively small way on schools and teachers. The inequality of educational opportunities is a matter that can be confronted wholesale only by state politics. Thus far, however, as we have seen before, state policies seem to drift away from, instead of towards, tackling it in earnest.

13

Indignation and swarm-like political groupings

Riccardo Mazzeo Almost fifteen years ago, in his most important book, *Self-Efficacy: The Exercise of Control*, Albert Bandura wrote:

> people do not live in social isolation, nor can they exercise control over major aspects of their lives entirely on their own. Many of the challenges of life center on common problems that require people to work together with a collective voice to change their lives for the better. The strength of families, communities, organizations, social institutions, and even nations lies partly in people's sense of collective efficacy that they can solve the problems they face. . . . Increasingly, people's lives are being shaped by powerful influences operating outside their traditional institutions and across lines of nation states. Widespread technological changes and globalization of economic forces are creating transnational interdependencies that place an increasing premium on the exercise of collective agency

to retain some measure of personal control over one's life course.[15]

As you sharply observed, the area for political action cannot be confined to the use of Facebook or Twitter, because it is only too easy to disconnect after what pretended to be engagement. The prevalence of tentative individual solutions tends to perpetuate the condition quo ante, but when individuals gather with their vibrant minds and *bodies* to protest against injustice putting their lives at stake, collective agency comes into play, and it's powerful, as we are confirming in Tunisia, in Egypt, in Syria.

As for school, something impressive is happening in Chile, where in the past Pinochet had reformed education in class-oriented terms with very expensive private schools and universities for the rich and public education, also expensive, for the others; families got more and more into debt to build a future for their children. During the last twenty years of democracy this system had not been changed, but in recent months the young have crowded together to claim the reform. President Piñera was subdued twice by the young president of the federation of university students, Camila Vallejo: first he had to dismiss his minister for education, and now he has just promised to reform the Constitution and to make a significant investment in schools and universities.

Zygmunt Bauman On 3 January 2011, John Lichfield reported in the *Independent*:

15 Albert Bandura, *Self-Efficacy: The Exercise of Control* (New York: W.H. Freeman, 1997), p. 477.

Indignez vous! (Cry Out!), a slim pamphlet by a wartime French resistance hero, Stéphane Hessel, is smashing all publishing records in France. The book urges the French, and everyone else, to recapture the wartime spirit of resistance to the Nazis by rejecting the 'insolent, selfish' power of money and markets and by defending the social 'values of modern democracy'. . . Mr Hessel and his small left-wing publisher (which is used to print runs in the hundreds) say that he has evidently struck a national and international nerve at a time of market tyranny, bankers' bonuses and budget threats to the survival of the post-war welfare state.

Three months later, on 13 April, Sudhir Hazareesingh confirmed in full the publisher's instincts. He wrote in the *Times Literary Supplement* that the 'slim pamphlet', which in the meantime had sold over 1 million copies in France alone and had been translated into more than ten European languages,

is a rousing call to reject apathy and engage in a 'peaceful insurrection' against all the injustices that blight the contemporary world: the continuing exploitation of the developing world by rich countries, the abuse of human rights by despotic governments, and the iron grip of mercantilism over the body politic, threatening the achievements in economic and social welfare for which his anti-fascist generation fought (and died).

The 'little pamphlet' was in fact a brochure rather than a book – only thirteen pages of text, sold for 3 euros a copy. The tiny size certainly helped to get the message through. For a generation trained on buzz-words, sound-bites, SMS and Twitter, this size was just short of off-putting; still legible and digestible, easily compressed into the habitual length of online comments; a kind of news eminently suited to being spread by word of mouth (or more to the point, by a hastily thumbed message from a mobile) and to quickly pass the critical point at which the 'Daniel Boorstin law' comes into operation (that bestsellers are the books that sell well because they are selling well).

This is not, of course, the full explanation – particularly in 2011, the year of the 'Arab Spring', of the amazing phenomenon of people taking to the streets and camping on the public squares of Spanish, Greek, Italian and Israeli cities. To put it in a nutshell, Hessel's seeds must have fallen on soil well prepared to make them sprout: people must already have been indignant for the call 'Indignez vous!' to be so avidly listened to – and heeded. Or to resort to another metaphor: the solution in which frustrations, betrayed hopes and dashed expectations were suspended, mixed with huge helpings of uncertainties, insecurities and fears of what the future held in store, must have been oversaturated for the slightest of shakes to have caused a massive sedimentation of what can be only called 'crystals of wrath'.

And what was it that prepared the soil and oversaturated the solution? In its briefest rendition, the answer is the widening gap between the rulers and the ruled. It gets ever more difficult to find out, let alone comprehend, the connection between the concerns brandished on high and the worries and anxieties of ordinary men and women further down (a reciprocal alienation covered up, from time to time, and each time briefly, by the attempts of governing bodies to shift the blame for the electorate's troubles away from themselves and onto imagined evildoers, like migrants...). State governments, stripped of much of their power by banks, multinational companies and other supranational forces, are unable to give serious attention to the genuine causes of people's misery, and people reply, as might be expected, by withdrawing their trust in the ability and will of governments to resolve their problems. Peter Drucker's famed declaration that there would no longer be salvation by society proved over the years to be a self-fulfilling prophecy. Desperately searching for salvation, people no longer look up, but around. And the young among us do so more than their elders; never in their short lives have they had a chance of expecting help from on high – let alone of having such expectations fulfilled.

The emergent politics, the hoped-for alternative to the discredited political mechanisms, tends to be horizontal and lateral, instead of vertical and hierarchical. I call it swarm-like: like swarms, political groupings and alliances are ephemeral creations, easily convened yet difficult to keep together for the time needed to 'institutionalize' (build lasting structures). They can do without headquarters, bureaucracy, leaders, foremen or corporals. They are brought together and disperse wellnigh spontaneously and with the same facility. Each moment of their life is intensely passionate, but intense passions are notorious for fading quickly. One cannot build an alternative society on passion alone, but the illusion of its feasibility consumes most of the energy that the building of such a society would require. Just to take up your example: I sincerely hope that Camila Vallejo's zeal won't be exhausted before Pinochet's gruesome inheritance is replaced by a fair and equitable educational model – but I fear that the chances of this happening are not particularly promising. My suspicion

(I pray to be proven wrong!) is that internet-mediated action can only achieve the replacement of unpolitics with an illusion of politics. . . Thus far, unfortunately, my suspicions are supported. None of the great, truly spectacular internet-prompted and electronically magnified explosions of grassroots protest has so far resulted in removing the grounds for the popular anger and despair. . .

14

Defective consumers and never-ending minefields

Riccardo Mazzeo   Yesterday (22 August 2011) I read in the *Guardian* the two opposing opinions of David Cameron and Tony Blair about the recent riots in England that resulted in 3,296 offences being committed, leading to 1,875 arrests and 1,073 people being charged: 'David Cameron reaffirmed his belief yesterday that the riots were symptomatic of moral decline in Britain, in contrast to Tony Blair who dismissed this argument as a "highfalutin' wail" that ignored the true cause of the problem'.

I think that both politicians speak (act) in bad faith. How on earth can Cameron declare: 'The greed and thuggery . . . did not come out of nowhere . . . There are deep problems in our society that have been growing for a long time: a decline in responsibility, a rise in selfishness, a growing sense that individual rights come before anything else"? As was underlined in the *Independent* by Howard Jacobson, winner of the Man Booker Prize for Fiction in 2010, 'that particular form of looting known as company theft keeps on raging unrestrained'.

The economic jackals are dragging the world to rack and ruin. Cameron tripled tuition fees. As for Blair, he said that to make this argument was 'to trash our own reputation abroad . . . Britain, as a whole, is not in the grip of some general moral decline'. Loretta Napoleoni gives the lie to the two English politicians in the last issue of the Italian weekly magazine *L'Espresso* (25 August 2011):

> In the British capital two societies live together, side by side: the marginalized, frustrated and furious one of the August riots, and the integrated, affluent and happy one that celebrated William and Kate last April. Here is summarized in the space of a couple of twitters the narrative, only apparently schizophrenic, of a nation very ingenuous in hiding its socio-economic contradictions. A country where for the last thirty years the racial divisions have overlapped the class ones, generating a social network that is nothing but the barbed wire of exclusion. An impregnable boundary between the haves and the have-nots who will never have.

I think you have something salient to say about the example of consumerism played nowadays among the young.

Zygmunt Bauman It would be wrong to describe the recent London unrest as a case of hunger or bread riots. These were riots of defective and disqualified consumers.

Revolutions are not the staple products of social inequality; but minefields are. Minefields are areas filled with randomly scattered explosives: one can be pretty sure that some of them will explode, sometime – but one can't say with any degree of certainty which ones and when. Since social revolutions are focused and targeted affairs, something can possibly be done to locate them and defuse them in time. Not minefield-explosions, though. Where minefields are laid out by the soldiers of one army, you can send other soldiers, from another army, to dig out the mines and disarm them; a dangerous job, if ever there was one – as the old soldier's wisdom goes on reminding us: 'the sapper makes only one mistake'. But where minefields are laid out by social inequality even this remedy, treacherous as it is, is unavailable: setting the mines and digging them up need to be done by the same army, which can neither stop adding new mines to the old nor avoid stepping on them – over and over again. Laying mines and falling victim to their explosions come in a package deal.

Social inequality always stems from the division between the haves and the have-nots, as Miguel Cervantes de Saavedra noted as early as half a millennium ago. But in different times it is the having or not having of *different* objects that are, respectively, the most passionately desired and the most passionately resented of positions. Two centuries ago in Europe, just a few decades ago in some places distant from Europe, and to this day in certain battlegrounds of tribal wars or playgrounds of dictatorships, the prime object that set the have-nots against the haves was bread or rice. Thanks to God, science, technology and certain reasonable political expedients this is now rarely the case. Which does not mean that the old division is dead and buried. Quite the contrary. . . The objects of desire whose absences are most violently resented have become many and varied – and their numbers, as well as the temptations they present, are growing by the day. And with them the wrath, humiliation, spite and grudges aroused by *not* having them – as well as the urge to destroy what you can't have. Looting shops and setting them on fire derive from the same impulse and gratify the same longing.

We are all consumers now, consumers first and foremost, consumers by right and by duty. Following the outrage of 11 September 2001, George W. Bush, calling on Americans to get over the trauma and go back to normal, said in effect, 'go back shopping'. It is the level of our shopping activity and the ease with which we dispose of one object of consumption in order to replace it with a 'new and improved' one which serves us as the prime measure of our social standing and score in the competition for life success. To all the problems we encounter on the path away from trouble and towards satisfaction we seek the solution in shops. From cradle to coffin we are trained and drilled to treat shops as pharmacies filled with drugs to cure or at least mitigate all the illnesses and afflictions in our lives and lives in common. Shops and shopping thereby acquire a fully and truly eschatological dimension. Supermarkets, as George Ritzer famously put it, are our temples; and, I may add, shopping lists are our breviaries, while strolls along shopping malls become our pilgrimages. Buying on impulse and getting rid of possessions no longer attractive enough in order to put more attractive ones in their place are our most stirring emotions. Fullness of consumer enjoyment means fullness of life. I shop, therefore I am. To shop or not to shop, this is the question.

For defective consumers, those contemporary have-nots, non-shopping is the jarring and festering stigma of a life unfulfilled – of nonentity and good-for-nothingness. It means not just the absence of pleasure, but the absence of human dignity. Of the meaning of life. Ultimately, of humanity and any other grounds for self-respect and the respect of the others around.

Supermarkets may be temples of worship for the members of the congregation. For those anathemized, found wanting and banished by the Church of Consumers, they are outposts of the enemy erected on the land of their exile. Those heavily guarded ramparts bar access to the goods which protect others from a similar fate: as George W. Bush would have to agree, they bar return (and for the youngsters who have never yet sat on a pew, access) to 'normality'. Steel gratings and blinds, CCTV cameras, security guards at the entrance and hidden inside, all add to the atmosphere of a battlefield and ongoing hostilities. Those armed and closely watched citadels of the enemy in our midst serve as a reminder, day in, day out, of the natives' misery, low worth and humiliation. Defiant in their haughty and arrogant inaccessibility, they seem to shout: I dare you! But dare you to what?

Shortly after the riots I was interviewed (electronically) by Fernando Duarte of the Brazilian paper *O Globo*. As it is closely related to your present question, let me quote his questions and my answers in full.

(1) *How much of an irony is the fact that the riots concentrated on the looting of consumer goods, given your body of work on postmodernism and consumerism?*

These riots were, so to speak, an explosion bound to happen sooner or later. Just as in a minefield, one knows that sooner or later some of the explosives will be true to their nature and explode, but one doesn't know where and when. In the case of a social minefield, however, an explosion is likely to spread instantaneously, thanks to the way contemporary technology transmits information in 'real time' and prompts the 'copy-cat' effect. This particular social minefield was created by the combination of consumerism with rising inequality. That was not a rebellion or an uprising of famished and impoverished people or of an oppressed ethnic or religious minority – it was a mutiny of defective and disqualified consumers, people offended and humiliated by the display of riches to which they are denied access. We have all been coerced and seduced into viewing shopping as the recipe for a good life and the principal solution of all life's problems – and then a large part of the population has been prevented from using that recipe. City riots in Britain are best understood as a revolt of frustrated consumers.

(2) *There are many arguments analysing the social roots behind the rioting and one inevitably has to analyse the inequality hypothesis. How tricky is the task for the establishment to address such questions when the concept of haves and have-nots seems to have shifted so much in the last few decades?*

Just like the reaction of governments to the economic depression caused by the credit collapse (that is, refinancing the banks in order to bring them 'back to normal': to the self-same activity that was the prime cause of the collapse and the depression!), the reaction of the British government thus far to the mutiny of the humiliated is bound to deepen the self-same humiliation that caused their rebellion – while leaving untouched the

sources of their humiliation, namely rampant consumerism combined with rising inequality. The hard-line,
high-handed measures taken by the government will
most probably shut down this explosion here and now,
but will do nothing to defuse the minefield that caused it
and to pre-empt further outbursts. Social problems were
never solved by the imposition of a curfew – they were
only left to rot and fester. The reaction of the British
government was a misguided attempt at a one-off,
instant solution to a long-term affliction of society. To
really tackle that kind of affliction would require nothing short of a serious reform of the ways society works,
and a genuine cultural revolution – something that
Edgar Morin suggested on his recent visit to São Paulo.

(3) *While talking to youths from poorer backgrounds,
there is clear resentment over the lack of opportunities
in education and work, but we have seen no universities burned, for example. Can we assume there is much
more symbolism in burning down a branch of Dixon's?*

Whatever else those youngsters may say when they are
pressed to explain why they are angry (mostly repeating the explanations they have heard on TV and read in
the papers. . .), the fact is that when they looted and set
shops on fire they did not attempt to 'change society',
to replace the present order with one that was more
humane and more hospitable to a decent and dignified life; they did not rebel against consumerism but
made a (misguided and doomed) attempt to join – if
only for a fleeting moment – the ranks of consumers
from which they have been excluded. Their mutiny was
an unplanned, unintegrated, spontaneous explosion of

accumulated frustration that can only be explained in terms of 'because of', not in terms of 'in order to'; I doubt whether the question of 'what for' played any role in that orgy of destruction.

(4) *How culpable are the public policies that created the council estates now described as pockets of apartheid?*

Successive British governments stopped building 'council estates' a long time ago. They left the spatial distribution of population, complete with its troubles and problems, entirely to market forces. Condensations of deprived people in certain areas of the city, not so different from the case of the favelas, are not guided by social policies, but by the price of housing, aided and abetted by the tendency of better-off sections of urban dwellers to lock themselves up, away from the city's troubles, in so called 'gated communities'. Segregation and polarization in cities today is the result of the free and politically uncontrolled play of market forces; if state policy makes its contribution, then it is only in the form of a governmental refusal to be bothered with responsibility for human welfare and its decision to 'contract it out' to private capital.

(5) *In your article for the journal* Social Europe, *you refuse to qualify the rioting as some kind of social revolution. Isn't there at least a whiff of a desire for social change in this situation, or is there just a massive imbalance between states of desire?*

So far I have failed to spot any evidence of such a desire. Romanticizing a humble life of self-denial has always been an ideology of the well-off and comfortable; as far as the collateral casualties of their comforts are concerned, however, they crave to imitate the well-off (an irrational dream, which can only be acted upon by irrational means!), not to replace their own lifestyle with one of self-restraint, temperance and moderation. As pointed out by Neal Lawson, the acute observer of present moods, 'what some have unhelpfully labeled a "feral underclass" is simply the mirror image of the now feral elite' – a distorted and distorting mirror, to be sure, but a mirror all the same. . .

(6) *The police won't be able to be on the streets in such large numbers for much longer and pretty soon life will be back to 'normal'. Given the relative success of the first consumer riots, how fearful of further trouble should Londoners be?*

Your guess is as good as mine. . . But we all know from abundant experience that punitive expeditions can only extinguish this or that local fire; but they aren't about to overhaul and rebuild the area currently going up in flames to stop it being 'socially inflammable' for ever. The sole effect of extemporary police action is to render the need for further police action still more pressing: police action, so to speak, excels in reproducing its own necessity. Remember that in the case of frustrated and disqualified consumers, bringing them back 'to normal' signifies returning them to a minefield-like condition!

(7) *Last but not least, and with a nod to the* New Statesman's *famous final question: given that consumerism is so ingrained in the postmodern society, is*

everyone doomed? How to address the 'shopping as normality scenario'?

A few months ago François Flahaut published a remarkable study of the idea of the common good and the realities for which it stands.[16] The major message of the new book, focused on the current shape of our radically 'individualized' society, is that the idea of human rights is currently used to replace and eliminate the concept of 'good politics' – while that idea, to be realistic, must be founded on the idea of the 'common good'. Human coexistence and social life constitute the good common to us all from which and thanks to which all cultural and social goods derive. The pursuit of happiness should for that reason focus on the promotion of experiences, institutions and other cultural and natural realities of life-in-common, instead of concentrating on indices of wealth, which tends to deform human togetherness into individual competitiveness and rivalry.

The point, therefore – and a point to which we don't yet have a convincing and empirically grounded answer – is whether the joys of conviviality are capable of replacing the pursuit of riches and the enjoyment of market-supplied consumables and one-upmanship, combining into the idea of infinite economic growth, in their role of well-nigh universally accepted recipes for the happy life. To put it in a nutshell, can our desire for the pleasures of conviviality, however 'natural', 'endemic' and 'spontaneous' they might be, be pursued inside the currently prevailing kind of society without

16 François Flahaut, *Où est passé le bien commun?* (Paris: Mille et Une Nuits, 2011).

falling into the trap of utilitarianism and bypassing the marketing mediation? Well, if we don't choose it by our own will, we may well be forced to accept it by the consequences of our refusal. . .

Professor Tim Jackson of the University of Surrey, in his book *Redefining Prosperity*, sounds the alarm: the present-day model of growth produces damage that is irreversible.[17] And this is because 'growth' is measured by the rise in material production, rather than services like leisure, health and education. . . Tim Jackson warns that by the end of this century 'our children and grand-children will face a hostile climate, depleted resources, the destruction of habitats, the decimation of species, food scarcities, mass migration and almost inevitably war'. Our debt-driven consumption, zealously abetted, assisted and boosted by the powers that be 'is unsustainable ecologically, problematic socially, and unstable economically'. Another of Jackson's several chilling observations – that in a social setting like ours, where the richest fifth of the world gets 74 per cent of the annual income of the planet while the poorest fifth has to settle for 2 per cent, the common ploy of justifying the devastation perpetuated by policies of economic growth by the noble need to put paid to poverty cannot be other than sheer hypocrisy and an offence to reason – has been almost universally ignored by the most popular (and effective) channels of information; or relegated, at best, to the pages and times of day known to host and accommodate voices reconciled and habituated to their plight of crying in wilderness.

17 Tim Jackson, *Prosperity Without Growth. Economics for a Finite Planet* (London: Taylor & Francis, Earthscan, 2009).

Jeremy Leggett (in the *Guardian* of 23 January 2010) follows Jackson's hints and suggests that a lasting (as opposed to doomed or downright suicidal) prosperity needs to be sought 'outside the conventional trappings of affluence' (and, let me add, outside the vicious circle of the use, misuse and abuse of products and energy): inside relationships, families, neighbourhoods, communities, meanings of life, and the admittedly misty and recondite area of 'vocations in a functional society that places value on the future'. Jackson himself opens his case with a sober admission that the questioning of economic growth is deemed to be the act of 'lunatics, idealists and revolutionaries', risking, fearing and expecting, not without reason, to be assigned to one or all three of these categories by the apostles and addicts of the grow-or-perish ideology.

In a market, as Adam Smith pointed out, we owe our daily supply of fresh bread to the baker's greed, not to his altruism, charity, benevolence or high moral standards. It is thanks to the all-too-human lust for profit that goods are brought to market stalls and that we can be sure to find them there. Even Amartya Sen, who insists that the well-being and freedom to lead decent human lives needs to be seen as the ultimate objective of the economy,[18] admits that 'it is indeed not possible to have a flourishing economy without extensive use of markets, so that the cultivation, rather than the prevention, of the development of necessary markets has to be a part of a prosperous and fair economic world'. What follows is, first, that to take away the lust for and chase after profit means making markets disappear, and goods together

18 See his essay 'Justice in the Global World', *Indigo* (winter 2011).

97

with them. Second, that markets being necessary for the 'economy to flourish', selfishness and avarice can be eliminated as human motives solely at our shared peril. Finally, there is a third conclusion: altruism is at logger-heads with a 'flourishing economy'. You can have one or the other, but hardly both of them together. . .

Jackson bypasses this quite serious hurdle by putting his wager on human reason and the power of persuasion; powerful weapons they both are, no doubt, and ones that would indeed be effective in a 'remodelling of the economic system' – were it not, however, for the unfortunate fact that the dictates of reason depend on the reality reasoned about, and that those realities, when reasoned about by reasonable agents, dispose of a 'power of persuasion' much stronger than any arguments ignoring them or playing them down. The reality in question is a society that can resolve (however imperfectly) the problems it itself creates (social conflicts and antagonisms menacing its own preservation) solely through an uninterrupted beefing up of the 'appetite for novelty' – thereby appealing to the greed and avarice that keep the economy 'flourishing'. . .

Jackson proposes a three-point programme: making people aware that economic growth has its limits; convincing (obliging?) capitalists to use as a guide in distributing their profits not only 'financial terms' but also social and environmental benefits to the community; and 'changing the social logic' used by governments in manipulating the arrangement of stimuli to induce people to expand and enrich their lives in other than a materialistic fashion. There is a snag, though: could all that be seriously contemplated without tackling those aspects of the human condition that prompted people to seek redress in the markets in the first place? That is, grievances that find no remedies, genuine or putative, and anxieties unattended to by society – which therefore find no other outlets than in the offers of the market and which are redirected to the consumer markets in an insistent even though vain and deceptive hope of finding a medicine or a solution?

15
Richard Sennett on difference

Riccardo Mazzeo What an illuminating analysis! The journalist Fabrizio Gatti, Birmingham correspondent for the Italian weekly *L'Espresso*, quotes you this week: 'One of the most insightful analyses of the riots, published by the sociologist Zygmunt Bauman, reveals: "The spatial arrangement of the population, together with its anxieties and problems, has been entirely unattended to, left to market forces. The concentration of deprived and poor inhabitants in particular areas of the city was not run by social policies, it was decided by the price of houses."' And he stresses that you don't talk of a 'broken society' as David Cameron does, but rather of 'gated communities'. Michela Marzano, in my opinion one of the most brilliant young philosophers, has described gated communities in an impressive manner:

> In a globalized world where borders have supposedly disappeared, there are classes of people who can live, work and travel within certain protected areas without ever being confronted with the rest of the world's population, in

particular with the most disadvantaged. How can we hope they will understand that they actually belong to the same humanity? Out of sight, out of mind. This entrenchment is obviously a way to overcome the fear of others, but the result is often the opposite of what was expected. Far from granting protection, barriers solidify differences, promote self-involvement and create more fear – the presence of walls brings about the idea that the enemy is everywhere, dangerous and nameless, and that all defensive measures are legitimate.

This is what Rodrigo Pla's *La Zona* (2008) shows. The film tells the story of three young Mexicans from a poor neighbourhood who enter a gated community protected by walls, surveilled by cameras and patrolled by a private security service. Access to the area is reserved to residents. The three youngsters break into a house and two of them end up killing the owner who caught them, but security intervenes immediately and kills two, while the third manages to escape. As he runs, he penetrates further into The Zone and the residents, instead of calling the police, decide to enforce justice on their own based on the state of exception that their closed community enjoys – they don't trust anybody but themselves, and whoever comes from outside is rejected as a threat. A cruel manhunt ensues and all those who express disagreement are treated first with suspicion and then with open hostility. All are caught in an infernal logic that allows no way out – the fugitive is not even considered a human being anymore and in the end, although innocent, he is ruthlessly executed.

La Zona talks about a fragmented, feudal society divided into two opposite sides who fear and hate each other. What can be done about a society where a minority is shamelessly rich and the other is desperately poor? Can we build walls so tall as to soothe the fear? Doesn't the isolation of all those who hide behind a wall generate even more terror? By surrounding themselves with walls the residents of the zone are responsible for their own imprisonment. Walls end up exacerbating the fear because they become the very materialization of separation from others. In this indifferent and cold world – where communities only obey their own rules, the only ones deemed able to preserve peace and safety – all is permitted. That's why any stranger is turned into an enemy to hunt down and kill.[19]

Gatti summarizes: 'After the dismantling of Al-Qaeda, the upper-class Englishmen who have never set foot in working-class estates now discover that the new enemies are the pupils, their teenagers. The solution is clear for everybody: we will need policy spending to strengthen the schools, to train the teachers, to help the companies to create jobs. A society to rebuild. But nowadays every policy investing in social growth will be punished by the stock exchange and by free-trade finance.'

Zygmunt Bauman   Ours is an increasingly diasporic society, and it is no wonder that many city residents feel apprehensive and threatened when they are exposed not just to strangers (city life has always meant being surrounded by strangers) but a new kind of strangers, never seen before, and therefore presumably 'undomesticated' and 'untamed', carrying unknown menace. The first 'gut' reaction is to withdraw into mini-fortresses called 'gated communities' and lock the doors; a demand to expel those strangers immediately follows, and all

19   Michela Marzano, *Le fascisme. Un encombrant retour?* (Paris: Larousse, 2008), pp. 174–6.

sorts of demagogues have a field day. Unless the process is counteracted, it acquires its own momentum and tends to reinforce itself: fear prompts people to refuse or break off communication with the ostensive carriers of the danger, and once communication is broken off the spectre of the alleged or imagined menace grows, which in turn renders the breakdown in communication still more defiant, radical and, in the end, absolute. In the absence of reciprocal communication there is little chance of submitting imagination to the test of practice – and almost no chance of working out a mutually satisfactory modus co-vivendi that will allow the city's cultural variety, now seen as liability, to be recast into an asset. I guess that education can do quite a lot to help cut this Gordian knot. . .

Pat Bertroche, running for the US Congress as a Republican in the state of Iowa, proposed on his blog (http://affordance.typepad.com) that illegal immigrants ought to have microprocessors grafted into their bodies: after all, he explained, I can graft a microprocessor into my dog if I want to be able to find it. Why not do the same to the illegals? Indeed, why?

In recent European reports from the scenes of massive clashes between pro-democratic protesters and the forces defending dictatorial regimes throughout the Arab world, two types of information took pride of place. One was the plight of the *citizens of those countries*: their lives were in danger; they should be moved to a safe distance from the trouble as soon as possible, spots from the southern to the northern coast of the Mediterranean; it was the government's most urgent task to make it happen, and any delay would be criminal. The other type of information was the danger that the northern coast of the Mediterranean would be flooded with the *refugees* running for their lives away from the battlefields of the civil wars raging on the southern coast; it was the government's most urgent task to stop it, and any delay would be criminal.

Similarly deep sighs of relief could be heard in the two simultaneously transmitted and reported news items from blood-soaked Libya: of the boat packed with British evacuees mooring at Valletta, and the crowds of Libyans running for shelter – but towards the Egyptian and Tunisian borders. The first reaction of the Italian government to the news of the change of regime in Tunisia was to send additional navy units to guard access to the Italian island of Lampedusa to stop Tunisian asylum seekers. . . And then François Fillon, the French prime minister, announced that France would send two planes with medical help to liberated Benghazi. Nice gesture, you might say, testimony to our solidarity with the gallant fighters for democracy, and our willingness to join them in the battle. You would say that – unless you read Fillon's own explanation: this is one of the measures to stop the wave of immigrants threatening to flood the Mediterranean countries; the best way to stop it is to make sure that the situation in Libya stabilizes soon.

It would be easy, but wrong, to explain these as extraordinary events or emergency measures. For almost two decades the policy of the Schengen countries on the northern side of the Mediterranean has been to 'subsidiarize' the detection and confinement of would-be immigrants inside their native countries or their immediate neighbours on the southern coast. In virtually every case, 'bilateral agreements' were signed or entered into unofficially with tyrannical and corrupt regimes, profiting – alongside the gangs of unscrupulous smugglers – from the misery of the impoverished and persecuted exiles, thousands of whom never managed to reach the other side of the sea in the overcrowded, unseaworthy dinghies supplied by gangsters.[20]

And yet one has to note that the customary strictness of the European immigration and asylum laws is currently growing stricter, and toughness of the stance taken towards prospective and successful asylum-seekers is growing tougher – all this unconnected with the unrest spreading from Tunisia to Bahrain. Commenting on the sudden hardening of Nicolas Sarkozy's posture towards aliens who had recently turned into Frenchmen or Frenchwomen, Eric Fassin, a distinguished anthropologist and sociologist, observed in *Le Monde* of 26 February 2011 that its purpose was to make all other Frenchmen and Frenchwomen 'forget the defeat of the President's policies on all fronts – from (falling) purchasing power to (rising) insecurity', and most particularly to use the politics of national identity as a cover for replacing social protection with a market-operated free-for-all.

Nothing new here, to be sure. The aliens inside (and particularly the settled ones) and the aliens at the gate (and particularly those who had good reason to be let through) have already been firmly fixed in the role of the usual suspects. Whenever another public inquiry is initiated about another misdeed, misdemeanour, failure

---

20 Among the most recent summaries of the state of the game immediately preceding the explosion of unrest in the Arab countries, see Alain Morice and Claire Rodier in *Le Monde Diplomatique*, June 2010.

or flop in governing circles, these aliens are the first to be brought to the police station and avidly filmed; they are shown on TV with the frequency of the memorable videos of the hijacked aircraft hitting the twin towers of the World Trade Centre. Soon after immigrant-generated internal security problems were picked on as the most urgent task of the French government came the decision to put the biggest of the bigwigs at the helm of the foreign affairs, interior affairs and defence departments. The meaning of the reshuffle was promptly spelled out by President Sarkozy in a way that left nothing to the imagination: 'My duty as the President of the Republic is to explain the future stakes, but above all to protect the present of the French' and this is why I've decided to 'reorganize the ministries dealing with our diplomacy and security'. And so persons have been appointed who are 'prepared to confront future events whose course no one can predict'.

In the good old days of 2004, when prices of stocks and real estate were climbing skywards by the day, GNP figures were rising up and those of unemployment were standing still, while the wallets in the pockets of the middle classes, and in the pockets of those hoping to join them, were swelling with credit cards, Nicolas Sarkozy's voice warmed up whenever he spoke of 'l'islam de France', of France's diversity, multiculturalism, even affirmative policy or positive discrimination, and their role in assuring peace and friendship in *les banlieues*. He would not hold with the populist habit of picking up Islam as a peculiarly suspect phenomenon demanding particularly watchful attention. In his *La République, les religions, l'espérance* (published in 2004), Sarkozy pointed out that Islam is one of the great religions, that the France of 2004 was no longer an exclusively Catholic country and that it had become a multicultural nation, so that instead of assimilation one should rather speak and worry about integration, a totally different kettle of fish. Unlike the now abandoned postulate of 'assimilation', the policy of integration does not require newcomers to renounce of what they are. Even in 2008, when dark clouds were already covering the notoriously blue French skies, the President, as Eric Fassin reminds us, emphatically condemned the principle of 'consanguinity', demanding that it be replaced with the principle of 'equality of opportunity' and pointing out that 'the best medicine against communitarianism' (*communautarisme*, in French discourse, is the concept of a population split into autonomous and partly self-enclosed and self-governing communities) 'is the Republic delivering on its promise'.

Well, it is an altogether different ball game now, to borrow an American idiom. It all started in early 2010 with the hue and cry after the Roma settled in Grenoble; Roma are, are they not, the first of the first among the usual suspects. But the Roma incidents proved to be just a modest *hors d'oeuvre;* mere appetizers. The presumption of symmetry between 'ceux qui arrivent' (the arrivals) and 'ceux qui accueillent' (their hosts) that used to underlie the pronouncements transmitted from governmental buildings has all but disappeared. No longer is respect required of both sides in equal measure. Respect is now due solely to France, and paying respect is the duty of the *accueillis* (the 'received') – received well or badly does not really matter. The French community (whatever that may mean), so the announcements state, does not want to change its way of living, its lifestyle.

But the unwritten condition that those 'received' will remain 'received' is that they do change their mode of life – whether they want to or not. And, in line with a habit already noted as the trademark of modern hypocrisy by that great Frenchman Albert Camus (whose personal contribution to the glory of France is second to none), the evil is once again done in the name of good, discrimination is promoted in the name of equality, and oppression in the name of freedom. For instance: 'We don't want to compromise on little girls' right to attend school'. . .

This is a thorny issue, no doubt. It is why the slogans of 'no tolerance to the enemies of tolerance' or 'no freedom to the enemies of freedom' sound so convincing. They do so because they take as an axiom what had still to be proved, because they pre-empt the question of whether the side whose condemnation and suppression that slogan is meant to legitimize are indeed guilty of the transgressions of which they stand accused, and because they omit the question of the right to prosecute as well as glossing over the illegal merging of the prosecutor's and the judge's roles. But does the prohibition of wearing headscarves in school indeed help to entrench 'little girls' right to attend school'?! André Grjebine of the Sciences Po–Centre D'Études et de Recherches Internationales, avers in the same issue of *Le Monde* that 'the alterity, perceived generally as a source of spiritual openness, can also be a carrier of fundamentalism, obscurantism and closure';[21] would he not agree, however, that his order of reasoning, with

---

21 André Grjebine, 'S'ouvrir à l'autre: oui. A son idéologie: non', *Le Monde*, 26 February 2011.

all its appearances of impartiality and of being *sine ira et studio*, is already a judgement in its own right, only disguised? He does not mention, after all, that spiritual closure, perceived by some as a carrier of identity and security, is all the same a source of fundamentalism and obscurantism – a connection at least as real as the one he preferred to put to the fore. Nor did he say that, much as the presence of spiritual openness in some may push some others to closure, it is the *absence* of spiritual openness that offers the invariable and infallible mark of every and any fundamentalism. More often than not, openness encourages, promotes and nourishes openness – whereas closure encourages, promotes and feeds closeness. . .

Amin Maalouf, the Lebanese author who writes in French and is settled in France, has considered the reaction of 'ethnic minorities', that is to say immigrants, to the conflicting cultural pressures they are subjected to in the country to which they have come. Maalouf's conclusion is that the more immigrants feel that the traditions of their original culture are respected in their adopted country, and the less they find themselves disliked, hated, rejected, frightened, discriminated against and kept at arm's length on account of their different identity, the more appealing the cultural options of the new country appear to them, and the less tightly do they hold on to their separateness. Maalouf's observations are, he suggests, of key importance to the future of intercultural dialogue. They confirm our previous suspicions and conjectures: that there is a strict correlation between the degree of perceived lack of threat on the one side, and the 'disarming' of the issue of cultural difference on the other – this as a result of overcoming impulses towards cultural separation, and a concomitant readiness to participate in the search for a common humanity.

All too often, it is a sense of being unwelcome and guilty without having committed a crime, of feeling threatened and uncertain (on both sides of the supposed frontline, among immigrants and indigenous population alike) that is the principal and most potent stimulant of mutual suspicion followed by separation and breakdown in communication: leading the theory of multiculturalism to degenerate into the reality of 'multicommunitarianism'. This is not a one-off trouble; it is a challenge we, and particularly the educationists among us, will have to cope with for a long time to come, because there is no prospect the influx of 'strangers' will slow down, let alone come to a halt – whatever is promised by politicians for the sake of winning the next election. . .

In a remarkable little study of one of the choices open to us, Richard Sennett suggests that 'informal, open-ended cooperation is how best to experience difference'.[22] Every word in this formula is crucial. As to the 'informality', it means that no rules of communication are fixed in advance; they are trusted to develop in their own way, because they are bound to change anyway as the communication grows in range, depth and substantiality: 'contacts between people of different skills or interests are rich when messy, weak when they become regulated'. 'Open-ended' means that the outcome should follow the (presumably protracted) communication, instead of being unilaterally fixed in

22 Richard Sennett, 'Humanism', *Hedgehog Review* (summer 2011), pp. 21–30.

advance: 'you want to find out what another person is about without knowing where it will lead; put another way, you want to avoid the iron rule of utility that established a fixed goal – a product, a policy objective – in advance'. And, finally, 'cooperation': 'You suppose that different parties all gain by exchanging, rather than one part gaining at the expense of others.' I would add: you need to accept that gaining in this particular game, like losing, is only conceivable *together*. Either we *all* gain, or we *all* lose. *Tertium non datur*.

Sennett sums up his recommendation in the following way: 'Offices and streets become inhumane when rigidity, utility and competition rule; they become humane when they promote informal, open-ended and cooperative interactions.'

I assume that all of us called to and wishing to teach can and should learn our strategy from that laconic yet comprehensive triune precept as articulated by Richard Sennett. Learn it ourselves in order to put it in operation – but also, and most importantly, transmit it to those called to and wishing to learn from us.

16

From Lacan's 'capitalist' to Bauman's 'consumerist'

Riccardo Mazzeo The move from Fordism – under which a worker would typically stay all his or her life with the same employer, living in the same town, with the same spouse – to the new paradigm of liquid modernity has caused, as you have shown in *Liquid Love* and in other writings, a transformation in the field of affective and sexual relations. Jacques Lacan in his 1969 speech in Milan theorized a switch from the Discourse of the Master – that, I think, corresponds to Fordism – to the Discourse of the Capitalist, where power dynamics are fragmented, dismembered, diffused, liquid, and where the antagonism of the master–slave dialectic (but also its stability and loyalty) gives way to the absolute power of the market. Today, women and men are adrift without any anchorage and there is no authority, however castrating, to give them a sense of direction. In this condition, individuals are faced with the task of reinventing themselves day by day in search of a means of salvation that they have to discover on their own.

The infinite freedom that individuals enjoy in our age marks an inversion of the ethical injunction – we are no longer asked to defer pleasure to build a better future for those who will come after us (Kant), but are instead incited to Enjoy Now (Sade). You have marvellously commented on this condition in *44 Letters from the Liquid Modern World*:

> This sort of 'impatience complex' was encapsulated a few decades ago in Margaret Thatcher's memorable complaint against the National Health Service, and her explanation of why she thought a free market for medical services to be an improvement: 'I want a doctor of my choice, at the time of my choice.' Shortly afterwards the tools – magic wands in the shape of a credit card – were invented, if not to make Thatcher's dream come exactly true, then at least to render it plausible and credible.[23]

This injunction to enjoy has pulverized love relationships as we have traditionally known them, while the elements of uncertainty, difficulty and risk that are part of courtship and of love stories worthy of their name have been discredited and are now considered a mere waste of time. Now we can order sex online by checking the menu of innumerable available lovers (as many as 2.5 million different opportunities, according to the website you mention):

> getting sex is now 'like ordering a pizza . . . now you can just go online and order genitalia'. Flirting or making passes are no longer needed, there is no need to work hard for a partners' approval, no need to lean over backwards in

---

23 Zygmunt Bauman, *44 Letters from the Liquid Modern World* (Cambridge: Polity, 2010), p. 23.

---

order to deserve and earn a partner's consent, to ingratiate oneself in her or his eyes, or to wait a long time, perhaps infinitely, for all those efforts to bring fruit.[24]

Obviously, after a certain amount of casual sexual encounters devoid of all poetry, one ends up feeling even more sad and lonely. It is this abysmal emptiness that, I believe, has generated what Massimo Recalcati has defined 'the new symptoms' which increasingly affect our children. In his book 'in praise of failure', Recalcati writes:

> [There is a] connection between the present epidemics and life in post-industrial societies founded on narcissism and the myth of consumption. Bulimia and anorexia represent the pathological expression of these two myths of our age. Bulimics manifest the pure myth of consumption – they swallow, chew and grind up everything. But binging proves the impossibility of filling up the hole that lies at the core of their being and reveals the deception that founds the Discourse of the Capitalist – everything can be purchased, except love. Love is a priceless gift, it is not an object launched on the market to be sold to the highest bidder, it is totally free. Anorexics, on the other hand, reject the logic of consumption. . . . They devote themselves to the narcissistic cult of the lean body. It is a private, autistic and antisocial cult, a deadly cult that leads to an irreversible weight loss. It's a perverse cult of self-image that affects not only the anorexic, but the whole social body. . . . This is the new historical form that the false market democracy takes on in the most advanced industrialized countries – the subject is literally stuffed with enjoyment,

24 Ibid., p. 22.

but at the same time it is pushed to consume more and more, so that consumption itself opens up the space for yet another pseudo-need. . . . this is what Lacan defines as the cunning of the Discourse of the Capitalist. What we are made to forget is that in human beings lack is not a deficit to correct, but the condition of all creation.[25]

This quotation resembles the way in which in 'Crowded solitude', the second of the 44 *Letters*, you defined our children's compulsion to be constantly connected with their peers on Facebook or Twitter as the atrophy of creativity: 'once you are always "on", you may never be fully and truly alone. And if you are never alone, then . . . "you're less likely to read a book for pleasure, to draw a picture, to stare out the window and imagine worlds others than your own"'.

The new symptoms are not limited to anorexia and bulimia; they also include substance abuse, depression and panic attacks. What they have in common is avoidance of a relationship to a human subject. Relationships with human beings are hard, risky and unpredictable, while attachment to objects is pacifying – whether it is a bottle, a dose of heroin, a line of cocaine, a designer's item, a fridge to assault or an iphone that stays connected with everybody. Objects are easy to get and just as easy to throw away.

Zygmunt Bauman   You are absolutely right – there is hardly anything in your exposition of the issue that I could, or would, question.

Just one more observation I feel like adding to your

25   Massimo Recalcati, *Elogio del fallimento* (Gardolo: Erickson, 2011), pp. 28–9.

argument: the war waged by the 'discourse of consumerism' (in my view, the proper description of the
phenomena you describe and we worry about – the
'discourse of capitalism' was quite different in the era
of the society of *producers*) is against any satisfaction
of human needs, desires, longings and ambitions that
does not pass by way of the shops – or is not mediated
by the purchase and use of commodities, and therefore
does not involve money changing hands (and political
discourse endorses that war, obliquely, when it measures the quality of society by its GDP figures). It even
militates against the pursuit of fun – to whose service it
allegedly devotes all its efforts and energy – if it bypasses
shopping malls on its way. Consumer markets expand,
thrive and profit by commodifying the pursuit of fun,
comfort and happiness; and that calls for demeaning,
stifling and extirpating all means of such a pursuit that
resist being diverted to a desire for commodities with a
price tag attached. . .

An aspect of the human condition that is particularly attractive to marketing experts (because it offers
apparently infinitely expanding opportunities) is the
ambivalence of human needs and desires (which you
illustrate so vividly when you quote Massimo Recalcati
on bulimia versus anorexia: the irreconcilability of two
equally overwhelming needs and desires, to devour
things and stay slim and fit – that is, in a position to
devour; a contradiction already known among the feast-
ing patricians in ancient Rome, described by Petronius
as using feathers to tickle their throats into vomiting to
clear their stomachs for still more delights of the palate).
Human nature is full of this kind of ambivalence.
Just a few off-the-cuff examples: security versus free-

dom, autonomy versus belonging, privacy versus social approval. . . In each pair of oppositions both values are indispensable, the snag being, however, that it is damned difficult to enhance one of them without damaging and diminishing the other. The closer we come to one pole of the opposition, the greater our desire grows to take a U-turn. We vacillate, tussle, flounce. . . a perpetual pendulum-like inclination to change direction, so to speak – and so also a fear of reaching a point of no return, of irrevocability. It seems that it is the hub of marketing tactics to play on that ambivalence. The greatest chance of capturing the attention of prospective clients and prompting them to shop is the promise that they can 'eat their cake and have it' (as English folk wisdom puts it); enjoy without fear of unwelcome consequences; or at least the offer is made of shifting the worry to a distant shelf, as in the insidious temptation to 'enjoy now, pay later', which bears no small responsibility for both the consumerist feast and the recent credit collapse.

All those tussles have consequences stretching far beyond individual inconvenience. Some of the most seminal relate to the weakening and impairment of interhuman bonds – not restricted to what you describe as the pulverization of love relationships. We all know the salutary and therapeutic aspects of the commodity markets only too well, and we know them from autopsy: from our own daily experience. We know the guilty feeling of being unable to spend enough time with our nearest and dearest, family and friends, to listen to their problems as attentively and compassionately as the problems require, to be 'always there for you', to be ready to abandon whatever we are doing at the moment and rush to help or just to share sorrows and offer consolation. If anything, these experiences are becoming ever more common in our hurried lives. Just one random illustration of the trend: where twenty years ago 60 per cent of American families had regular family dinners, now only 20 per cent of American families now meet around the dinner table.

Most of us are overwhelmed by the worries arising from our daily relations with bosses, workmates or clients, and most of us take those worries with us wherever we go, in our laptops and mobile phones – to our homes, weekend strolls, holiday hotels: we are never further than a phone call or a text message from the office, constantly at its beck and call. Connected perpetually to the office network as we are, we have no excuse for not using Saturdays and Sundays for completing the report or the project ready to be delivered on the Monday. 'Closing time' never arrives at the office. The once sacrosanct border separating home from office, work time from 'free time' or 'time of leisure', has been all but effaced, and so each and every moment of life becomes a moment of choice – a grave choice, a painful and often seminal choice, a choice between career and moral obligations, work duties and the demands of all those people who need our time, compassion, care, help and succour.

Obviously, consumer markets won't resolve those dilemmas for us, let alone chase them away or render them null and void; and we don't expect them to. But they can, and are, eager to help us to mitigate and even to quash the pangs of guilty conscience. They do it through the precious, exciting gifts on offer, which you can spy out in the shops or on the internet, buy and use to make some of those people hungry for your love smile and rejoice – if only for a brief moment. We are trained to expect shop-supplied gifts to compensate those people for all those face-to-face, hand-in-hand hours we should have offered them but didn't; the more expensive those gifts are, the greater the compensation they are expected by the giver to offer to their recipients, and consequently the stronger their placating and tranquillizing impact on the giver's pangs of conscience.

Shopping thereby becomes a sort of moral act (and vice versa: moral acts lead through the shops). Emptying your wallet or debiting your credit card takes the place of the self-abandonment and self-sacrifice that the moral responsibility for the Other requires. The side-effect, of course, is that by advertising and delivering commercialized moral painkillers, consumer markets only facilitate, instead of preventing, the fading, wilting and crumbling of interhuman bonds. Rather than helping to resist the forces that make the bonds fall to dust, they collaborate in the work of their emaciation and gradual destruction.

Just as physical pain signals organic trouble and prompts urgent remedial action, moral scruples signal the dangers threatening interhuman bonds – and would prompt deeper reflection and more energetic and adequate action were they not tempered by the moral tranquillizers and painkillers supplied by the market. Our intentions to do good to others have been commercialized. And yet it is not the consumer markets that need to be charged with the main responsibility, let alone the sole responsibility, for that having happened. By design or by default, consumer markets are *accessories* to the crime of causing interhuman bonds to fall apart: accessories both before and after that crime is committed. . .

If the level of consumption determined by biological and social survival is by its nature stable, the levels required to gratify the other needs promised, expected and demanded to be serviced by consumption are, again by the nature of such needs, inherently oriented upwards, and rising; the satisfaction of those added needs does not depend on maintaining stable standards, but on the speed and degree of their rise. Consumers turning to the commodity market in search of satisfaction for their moral impulses and fulfilment of their duties of self-identification (read, self-commodification) are obliged to seek differentials in value and volume, so this kind of 'consumer demand' is an overpowering and irresistible factor in the upward push. Just as the ethical responsibility for Others tolerates no limits, consumption invested with the task of venting and satisfying moral impulses is not tolerant of any kind of constraint imposed on its extension. Having been harnessed to the consumerist economy, moral impulses and ethical responsibilities are recycled, ironically, into an awesome hindrance when humanity finds itself confronted with arguably the most formidable threat to its survival: a threat which, in order to be fought back against, will need a lot, perhaps an unprecedented amount, of voluntary self-constraint and readiness for self-sacrifice.

17
Žižek and Morin on monotheism

Riccardo Mazzeo In the last eleven years, I have read six books and innumerable articles by Slavoj Žižek, in my opinion a very interesting, though not always convincing, Lacanian philosopher, and this is the first time I have found your name quoted by this bizarre and talented thinker. It happened in his article 'Shoplifters of the World Unite', published on 19 August 2011 in the *London Review of Books*, where he discusses the meaning of the recent riots. At the beginning his analysis is appropriate:

> We are told again and again that we are living through a debt crisis, and that we all have to share the burden and tighten our belts. All, that is, except the (very) rich. The idea of taxing them more is taboo: if we did, the argument runs, the rich would have no incentive to invest, fewer jobs would be created and we would all suffer. The only way to save ourselves from hard times is for the poor to get poorer and the rich to get richer. What should the poor do? What *can* they do?

Žižek is very insightful when he explains the weakness of both the Conservative reaction, predictably embodied by Cameron's position, and the no less predictable naive leftist liberal one. He finally comes to the point:

> Zygmunt Bauman characterized the riots as acts of 'defective and disqualified consumers': more than anything else, they were a manifestation of a consumerist desire violently enacted when unable to realize itself in the 'proper' way – by shopping. As such, they also contain a moment of genuine protest, in the form of an ironic response to consumerist ideology: 'You call on us to consume while simultaneously depriving us of the means to do it properly – so here we are doing it the only way we can!' The riots are a demonstration of the material force of ideology – so much, perhaps, for the 'post-ideological society'. From a revolutionary point of view, the problem with the riots is not the violence as such, but the fact that the violence is not truly self-assertive. It is impotent rage and despair masked as a display of force; it is envy masked as triumphant carnival.

Žižek also agrees with you about the *indignados* who lack 'a positive program of sociopolitical change. They express a spirit of revolt without revolution'.

I don't agree with Žižek anymore where he defines the riots as a 'passage à l'acte' and says that religion, in so far as it provides 'absolute Meaning', engenders terrorism. I am an agnostic but I believe that our cynical epoch would benefit from some transcendence, some religious sense that does not necessarily imply fanaticism and that is not even strictly a 'religion'. As Edgar Morin puts it:

> The point is to create a dialogue between faith and uncertainty. I'm not talking about religious faith, as I don't

believe in any creed, but about a faith in values, a faith in the possibility of improving human relations – a faith in the value of fraternity. I think that this type of faith cannot be proved scientifically because nothing guarantees that its efforts will succeed. . . . I have given as an example the mating of whales the way our great Michelet described it. He imagined that for two whales to mate, the female and the male had to simultaneously rise vertically so that for a brief moment the genital organ of the male could encounter that of the female. The whales would try many times unsuccessfully until finally they would manage to copulate.

I have chosen this metaphor because I feel that in the domain of ethics and of social and political life, we have to act this way, with enormous efforts and waste of semen, in order to finally obtain a result! And a result cannot be taken for granted, but we have to try, at the ethical level, to do like the whales.[26]

Zygmunt Bauman   Just to clarify the question: a polytheist can also be a deeply religious person – the ancient Romans' Pantheon was filled to the brim with gods, more and more of them year by year, as new provinces kept being added to the expanding Roman Empire. . . What is tacitly assumed by both Žižek and Morin in the statements you quote, as well as by all or most of their readers, is the *monotheistic* nature of religion, not religion *as such*; that means the attitudes specific to the three 'world religions', all descending from Jerusalem. Well, for all three of them 'coming to a consensus' would call for the abandonment and betrayal of faith, since their kind of faith rests on the assumption of a one

---

26   Edgar Morin, *Ma gauche* (Paris: Bourin, 2010), p. 130.

---

and only God. This assumption justifies the Michelet/
Morin allegory of sex among whales, particularly when
religiously agnostic people try to comprehend and make
intelligible the conduct of the religious others. But one
can imagine coming to a kind of consensus that involves
permission to remain loyal to the respective gods of the
consenting; an acceptance that the differences between
religious faiths do not stand in the way of good will in
a peaceful and mutually beneficial cohabitation. By the
way, people of all three monotheistic denominations
participated in the looting of the London supermarkets without cutting each other's throats and without
fighting over the spoils. . . Must we assume that the
experience of cooperation in spite of their monotheisms
in that gruesome variety of action over a 'mono-issue'
cannot be extended to nobler and more praiseworthy
causes?

I would remind us at this point of Sennett's 'informal, open-ended cooperation', a fully realistic model of
collaborative communication entered into without pre-
sumptions and without putting the cart before the horse
– that is, the final resolution before the debate. After all,
both talking to each other and shooting each other can
be compared to the excruciatingly tortuous and risky
fate of the sex-hungry whales. Both stances call for
tremendous effort and both stop short of guaranteeing
success, and their respective merits should be measured
by criteria other than the arduousness of the task and
the likelihood of success.

Another comment, on the margin: the movement of
the *indignados* is indeed in some cases (as in the London
riots) a 'revolt without revolution'; but on the whole,
as a phenomenon of 'direct' or 'unmediated' vindica-

tion, it seems to evolve towards a 'revolution without revolutionaries'. . . . They take the status quo, so to speak, 'at its word', and so confront it with the full volume of the ambitions it inspires and officially endorses – a volume which far exceeds its powers to support it. And so the demands, altogether non-revolutionary in themselves, are bound to accomplish a truly revolutionary feat: to discredit the status quo, lay bare its impotence, and thereby prompt its collapse.

18

Proust's petite madeleine and *consumerism*

Riccardo Mazzeo   On 2 September 2011, I came to see the talk you gave at the conference in Sarzana, the Festival della Mente. It has always been exciting to listen to you, and the rest of the audience obviously felt the same because you got many rounds of applause and at the end the applause broke out like a powerful, liberating, purifying rainstorm.

This time I noticed a change of style – you talked about the social networks as a huge innovation that, like Jesus Christ's multiplication of the loaves and fish, suddenly makes abundant and even unlimited what was once painfully sparse and difficult. On the new social scene, a mass of individuals has left the kitchen table around which they shared supper with their family and has frantically embraced new gadgets, designer clothing and loneliness. This mass of individuals has now discovered how to make 'friends' on Facebook.

You didn't lash out at this useless proliferation of contacts that have nothing to do with authentic human relationships. You said that you are not a prophet and that it is up to us to decide whether it is better to live in an old-style community that demands commitment and devotion from its members and that they cannot abandon without being branded with the mark of shame and disgrace, or this new modality of social interaction that can be suspended by simply pressing the appropriate delete icon. You have always been Socratic, but this suspension of judgement and your concern for all the human beings who read your essays and listen to your talks inflamed the atmosphere; at the end of your speech, almost magically, a thunderstorm broke out, no doubt urging us to come out of this impasse, to stop the Sisyphean torture and end the logic of senseless consumption that produces even more consumption and waste. We have to fight against the marketing experts, who, for example – and I read this in yesterday's newspaper (*La Stampa*, 5 September 2011) – have devised yet another strategy of persuasion consisting in creating artificial incenses that give off the flavours of the simple and appetizing foods of our childhood.

Thanks to nebulization technology, the Brooklyn supermarket chain Netcost has increased sales by 5 per cent in the last three months. But the most impressive success has been Nike's, which has had an 80 per cent increase in sales. Claudio Risé, a psychotherapist and the author of *Guarda, tocca, vivi* (Look, Touch, Live),[27] says that stimulating the senses is the last resource to move consumers who have become impermeable to all other marketing techniques, citing 'the ever new hunting territories' you mentioned in *Does Ethics Have a Chance in a World of Consumers?* And, really, what

---

27 Claudio Risé, *Guarda, tocca, vivi* (Milan: Sperling & Kupfer, 2011).

other opportunities do we have if even Proust's *petite madeleine* is exploited as the last resort to reinforce our personal identity as dumb and gullible consumers?

Zygmunt Bauman Pleasure, comfort, convenience and reduction of effort – instantaneity of satisfaction, dreams turning into reality and softening the cumbersome realities enough for them to be dismissed as dreams (or phantoms, or figments of phantasy) – these are the promises, the wagers, the stratagems of an economy driven by greed and operated through shopping. The making and unmaking of friends is only one instance of a universally applied strategy. You rightly put it alongside the latest promise, this time of making the sweet memories of childhood available (in shops, obviously) on demand: no more laborious '*searching for times lost*', as a matter of fact no more *times lost*, no more need of a Proust-like genius to find, resurrect and recuperate them – a credit card will do nicely, thank you!

Are we, contrived consumers, gullible? Most probably we are. But dumb? Not necessarily. Who in their sane mind wouldn't prefer effortlessness over hard effort? The consumerist promise arrived on the crest of centuries-long longings; a false promise it might be, deceitful and misleading, but in no way is it unattractive and it is certainly not out of tune with a 'natural predisposition' (Freud pinpointed inborn human sloth as one of the main reasons for the need for coercion; stripped of coercive powers, the marketing masterminds have managed to substitute seduction for coercion). The consumerist temptation is intended as a spur to action – or, more precisely, as a deflection of activity, that antonym of sloth, towards servicing what is profit-making, instead of eliciting routine and discipline, which was the principal aim of coercion. Submission to consumerist temptations is an act of voluntary servitude. It is, to use a new-fangled expression, 'pro-active': it presumes choice and positive action. Which is, perhaps, what renders the trap so exceptionally difficult to resist and still more to disarm. After all, a consuming life is lived as a supreme expression of autonomy, authenticity and self-assertion – the attributes (indeed, modalities) sine qua non of the sovereign subject. It is for that reason that a consumerist orientation consumes (or at least heavily taxes) the life energy that could be deployed in the service of those other human concerns on behalf of which you appeal – commitment, devotion, responsibility. . .

19
On fuels, sparks and fires

Riccardo Mazzeo Last week, on Saturday, 10
September, I went with my wife and daughter to the
town of Rovereto to protest against the bicycle race,
the Padania Tour. I hadn't been part of a crowd invad-
ing a street or a square for a long time, but in this case
my family was going to participate anyway and I didn't
want them to be there without me, and I absolutely
agreed with the rebellion against the racist Lega party
that wants so-called Padania to be recognized as a special, different, *better* part of Italy. No longer being used
to this kind of mostly youthful experience, and trying
to remember what Canetti wrote in *Masse und Macht*
about crowds, I felt like an entomologist, and my young
daughter pointed out that my sober clothes, my Ray-Ban
sunglasses and the five newspapers under my arm made
me look like an undercover agent. In front of the lines
of anti-riot police, we were highly differentiated: young
aggressive extreme leftists, our determined but moderate
'partisan' (anti-fascist) association, some communists,
and even the very colourful Mazzinians (followers of

Mazzini – raised from the dead). Three hours later there was a little fight with the police, a baton charge against the protesters' frontline, but the cyclists' route was changed and we could feel satisfied with this result.

I tell you this negligible story because squares are being invaded anywhere: what do you think of this sort of 'Spring'?

Zygmunt Bauman   'The Arab Spring triggers popular rebellions against autocrats across the Arab world. The Israeli Summer brings 250,000 Israelis into the streets, protesting the lack of affordable housing and the way their country is now dominated by an oligopoly of crony capitalists. From Athens to Barcelona, European town squares are being taken over by young people railing against unemployment and the injustice of yawning income gaps' – so writes Thomas L. Friedman of the *New York Times*.[28]

People have taken to the streets. And public squares. First on Prague's Vaclavske Namesti, way back in 1989, and right after in one capital of the Soviet bloc countries after another. Then, famously, on the main city square in Kiev. In all those places, and some others as well, new habits started to be tested: no longer a march, a demo going from a gathering point to a destination; rather, a permanent occupation of sorts, or a siege lasting for as long as the demands are not met.

After the trying and the testing, the new mode has recently turned into a norm. People have tended to settle in public squares with the clear intention of

---

28 Thomas L. Friedman, 'A Theory of Everything (sort of)', *New York Times*, 13 August 2011.

staying there for quite a while – for as long as it takes to achieve or be granted whatever it is they want. They have taken tents and sleeping bags with them to show their determination. Others have come and gone, but regularly: every day or evening, or once a week. What did they do once they were on the square? They listened to speeches, applauded or booed, carried billboards or banners, shouted or sang. They wanted something to change. In each case, that 'something' was different. No one knew for sure whether it meant the same for everyone around. For many, its meaning was anything but crystal clear. But whatever that 'something' was, they savoured the change already occurring: staying on Rothschild or Tahrir square day and night, surrounded by crowds evidently tuned in to the same wavelength of emotions, it was such a change, actually happening and being enjoyed. Rehearsed verbally on Facebook and Twitter, it was now finally being experienced in the flesh. And without losing the traits that made it so endearing when it was practised on the web: the ability to enjoy the present without mortgaging the future, rights without obligations.

The breathtakingly intoxicating experience of togetherness; perhaps, who knows, solidarity. That change, already occurring, means: each person is no longer alone. And it took so little effort to accomplish it, little more than pushing in a 'd' instead of the 't' in that nasty word 'solitary'. Solidarity on demand, and lasting as long as the demand endures (and not a minute longer). Solidarity not so much in sharing the cause chosen as solidarity in having a cause; I and you and all the rest of us ('us', the people on the square) having a purpose, and life having a meaning.

On fuels, sparks and fires

Not all the people taking to the streets enter the square and stay there. The experience of 'all of us in it' may be more like a flash in an overheated pan than a pilgrimage – and in London, Birmingham, Manchester or Bristol it was for a little while. No pretence at a cause. No time for solidarity. No longing for a meaning – fun will do nicely, thank you very much. Joy to be consumed on the spot. Fulfilment now. Instantaneous satisfaction. Is not that what the life of consumers is about? Four teenagers who looted in neighbourhoods across London told Sky News that it was like a 'shopping spree'.[29] A shopping spree, indeed. The only difference from other shopping sprees was the absence of cash and credit cards: a shopping spree made to the measure of people who have neither.

One of the foremost metaphors for a crowd (both a 'moving' and a 'stationary' crowd) is, according to Elias Canetti, fire. And no wonder: fires warm up, just like the cosiness of belonging; sometimes, however, they get too hot for comfort, burst into flames without warning, run out of control and burn – as crowds all too often do. The fuels that can be used to keep the fire alive differ from one to the other. All fuels are inflammable, but when they are ignited, some smoulder quietly and glow; others, however, will explode from a single spark.

To return from the fire metaphor to what it stands for, the crowds flowing through the streets into the city square: some of them come primed to explode, others are suited to quiet yet protracted smouldering. True, both need a spark to kindle or ignite them; what follows the ignition, however, is not determined by the spark,

29 Sky News, 12 August 2011.

but by the properties of the combustibles – even though different kinds of sparks may attract different kinds of crowds. With the advent of portable means of instant mass communication, sparks will go on flying, but it is not the electronic devices, however smart, that determine the incidence and the nature of social explosions. Just how little is understood by the people responsible for the massive production and accumulation of explosives (most prominently, the rampant, blatant, dehumanizing social inequality and massive production of disqualified consumers in the midst of a society of consumers) or desired to be understood. What moves and guides the society entrusted to their care is demonstrated by David Cameron's idea of switching off social websites in order to save shops from being burnt and looted. . .

Friedman suggests: 'There are multiple and different reasons for these explosions, but to the extent they might have a common denominator I think it can be found in one of the slogans of Israel's middle-class uprising: "We are fighting for an accessible future." Across the world, a lot of middle- and lower-middle-class people now feel that the "future" is out of their grasp, and they are letting their leaders know it.' He sums up his diagnosis and his recommendations:

> We are increasingly taking easy credit, routine work and government jobs and entitlements away from the middle class – at a time when it takes more skill to get and hold a decent job, at a time when citizens have more access to media to organize, protest and challenge authority and at a time when this same merger of globalization and IT is creating huge wages for people with global skills (or for those who learn to game the system and get access to

money, monopolies or government contracts by being close to those in power) – thus widening income gaps and fueling resentments even more.[30]

He may be right. . .

Clearly, the world as we knew it, or thought we knew it, is going out of joint. It is accelerating daily, and in real time getting shorter day by day. The old certainties have disappeared. The old remedies don't work. The old and trusty drawing boards lie idle or keep turning out endless copies of old blueprints, as in a somnambulist trance. Hopes seem only to find shelter in the tents pitched on public squares. . .

Tents full of sound and fury in search of signification. . .

30   Thomas A. Friedman, 'A Theory of Everything (sort of)'.

20

On glocalization coming of age

Riccardo Mazzeo This is our last conversation, my dear Zygmunt. Today is 19 September 2011 and we talked about this in Modena three days ago, before your two latest conferences, one in Sassuolo on 'What is left of nature' and the other in Pordenone titled 'Aren't we all migrants?'. I have never seen you as often as in these last months, and from your two talks I have drawn so many notions that I would like to expand on them, but I fear that they wouldn't fit on this page, the last one I am going to write to you. So I will just focus on a couple of things. The first one is the sense of guilt that, as you said, permeates our relationship with our families. As we neglect our partners and children to pursue our careers, marketing experts capitalize on our guilt by directing us towards forms of compensation (from the latest model of cellphone or iPhone to designer shoes or bags) which always involve buying something. We spend a lot of money on gifts we bring our loved ones on the days we finally get to see them. The result is that we have even less time to spend with our family – we have to work harder and earn more money to afford more expensive gifts. This is a vicious circle that could easily be redressed if we offered our presence, attention and care instead of objects. As you pointed out, if Freud were alive today he would have to rewrite *Civilization and its Discontents*, taking into account the fact that our culture no longer encourages us to repress and delay pleasure, but instead urges us to enjoy freely all the pleasure and goods our consumer society can provide.

A great Italian intellectual, Marco Belpoliti, in his book *Senza vergogna* (Without Shame), refers to Alain Ehrenberg to introduce the idea of 'amoral shame'. You did the same in 44 *Letters*.

> The growing insecurity about personal identity typical of postmodern society and the constant humiliations our self image is subjected to cause what Alain Ehrenberg has called 'the strain of being oneself'. We have moved from a society based on obedience and discipline to a society that values unconventionality and promotes the belief that, at all levels, *everything is possible*. Oedipus, the symbol of patriarchal society, and the typically bourgeois sense of guilt, is replaced by vanity, i.e. by Narcissus and its fascination with the mirror. Narcissus brings freedom, but also a growing sense of emptiness and impotence.[31]

My second observation draws on the text by Kant you analysed in your fascinating book *Society under Siege* – the text is *Idea for a Universal History from a Cosmopolitan Point of View* (1784). There Kant says that since our world is a sphere, 'a certain distance cannot be increased indefinitely without nullifying it'.

31 Marco Belpoliti, *Senza vergogna* (Parma: Guanda, 2010), p. 22.

The surface of the globe on which we live doesn't allow an 'infinite dispersion' – at the end we will all be neighbours simply because there is nowhere else to go. So in the end we will all have to put up with one another and live together.

I believe that moment has arrived: today the global borders on the local, and the other way round. Mick Jagger, the lead singer of Rolling Stones, has just started a new supergroup with Dave Stewart from Eurythmics, young soul singer Joss Stone, the reggae king Damian Marley, and the Academy Award winning Indian composer A. R. Rahman. I saw their first video and I was pleased to notice that it didn't show the usual frantic changes of settings, costumes and hairdos, or the habitual array of sculpted and scantily dressed female and male dancers. In the video, we only see musicians with different voices, ethnic origins and looks singing together, each preserving their own singularity and musical style. It may be just one more successful marketing operation, but this made me think about those groups of children who in our first conversation you said you used to see from your window as they were coming home from school. Each group of children forty years ago would all have had the same skin colour; today they are all different.

Zygmunt Bauman One is tempted to say that social inventions or reinventions (like the newly invented or rediscovered possibility of restoring to city squares their ancient role of the agora where rules and rulers were made and unmade) tend to spread 'like a forest fire'. One would say that were it not for the fact that globalization has finally invalidated that time-honoured

On glocalization coming of age

metaphor. Forest fires proceed by *spreading*. Today's social inventions progress by *leaping*.

In order to explain what I have in mind, let me recall one of the less hyped aspects of the recent, though already half-forgotten experience of the 'Arab Spring'. . .

What we can and should learn from that experience is that geographical distances no longer matter. Distances are no longer obstacles, and their lengths no longer determine the distribution of probabilities. Neither do neighbourhoods and physical proximity – this is why the metaphor of the 'domino effect', implying close proximity, indeed a contiguity of cause and effect, is losing much, perhaps even most, of its accuracy. Stimuli travel independently of their causes: causes may be local, but the reach of their inspiration is global; causes may be global, but their impacts are shaped and targeted locally. Entangled in the world wide web, copycat patterns fly round extraterritorial space almost randomly – without scheduled itineraries and encountering few if any barriers or checkpoints – but they invariably come down on locally built landing strips. You can never be sure in advance on which strip they will land, by which of the innumerable control towers they will be spotted, intercepted and guided to the local airfield, and how many crash landings they will suffer and where. What makes prediction a waste of time, and prognoses unreliable, is the fact that the landing strips and control towers share those floating patterns – they are constructed ad hoc, to catch a single selected trophy, hunt after one quarry, and they tend to shut down the moment the mission has been accomplished. Who is that 'Al-Chahid' ('Martyr' in Arabic) who single-handedly summoned the crowds to transform Tahrir Square for a few days into a (temporary, ad hoc) agora? No one had heard about her or him before (read, she or he was not there before), and no one recognized the woman or man on the square beyond the nickname (read, she or he was not there) when the crowds answered her call. . . The point is, though, that this hardly matters.

The distinction between far away and close by, or here and there, have been made virtually null and void with the transfer to cyberspace and subjection to online or on-air logic in their pragmatic potency, if not in the imagination, which can lag sluggishly behind. This is the condition that *glocalization*, the process of stripping locality of its importance while simultaneously adding to its significance, was aiming for from its very start. The time has come to admit that it has arrived there: or, rather, that (pushing or pulling) it has brought us there.

Stripping place of its *importance* means that place can no longer consider its own plight and potency, fullness or emptiness, the dramas played out in it and the spectators they attract, as its private matter. Places can (and do) propose, but it is now the turn of the unknown, uncontrolled, intractable and unpredictable forces roaming in the 'space of flows' to dispose. Initiatives are still local, but their consequences are now global, staying stubbornly out of the reach of the predicting, planning and steering powers of their birthplace, or any other place for that matter. Once launched, they – like the notorious 'intelligent missiles' – are fully and truly on their own. They are also 'hostages to fate' – though the fate holding them hostage is nowadays composed and perpetually recomposed from the ongoing rivalry between local landing strips, hastily paved, for those ready-made copycat patterns. . . The current map or rankings of the established airports are of no importance here. Also of no importance would be the composition of the global air traffic authority, were such an institution in existence – which it is not – which pretenders to that role are learning the hard way.

'Every time the administration uttered something, its words were immediately overtaken by events on the ground,' said Robert Malley, Middle East and North Africa programme director for the International Crisis Group, quoted by the *New York Times*. 'And in a matter of days, every assumption about the United States's relationship with Egypt was upended.' And according to information about Egypt reported by Mark Mardell, the BBC's North America editor, 'US Secretary of State Hillary Clinton has telephoned the new vice-president and intelligence chief of two decades, Omar Suleiman, to tell him immediately to seize the opportunity for a transition to a more democratic society. That transition must start now. She said that the violence was shocking and told him that they must investigate the violence and hold those responsible accountable.' A few hours later, leaders of the countries believed to be the most important places in Europe – Merkel, Sarkozy, Cameron, Zapatero and Berlusconi – in an uncharacteristically unanimous declaration, repeated Hillary Clinton's appeal/demand. They all said what they did at roughly the same time that Al-Jazeera's cameras caught a demonstrator carrying a placard reading 'Obama, shut up!'. . . The *significance* of a place, rising counter to its importance, is precisely in its ability to accommodate the carrying of such placards and the people to carry them. Hands too short to meddle with things in global space reach just far enough (or at least seem to reach far enough) to embrace the locality and press it close, while (hopefully) pushing away intruders and false pretenders.

One day after Hillary Clinton's announcement, the *New York Times* reported a full recasting of American foreign policy: 'The Obama administration seemed determined Wednesday to put as much daylight as possible between Mr Obama and Mr Mubarak, once considered an unshakable American supporter in a tumultuous region.' Well, that global power would hardly have made such an acrobatic volte-face had not that distant locality decided to make use of its newly found significance. . . As Shawki al-Qadi, a lawmaker and opposition figure in Yemen, suggested, it was not that the people were afraid of their governments, which had surrendered their powers to 'global forces' in exchange for being freed of their obligations to their own people; as he put it, 'It is the opposite. Governments and their security forces are afraid of the people now. The new generation, the generation of the Internet, is fearless. They want their full rights, and they want life, a dignified life.' The knowledge that governments, in the form into which they have been squeezed by 'global forces', are not a protection against instability, but instability's principal cause, has been forced into the heads of the self-appointed 'world leaders' by the spectacular display of glocalization's illogical logic in action.

'Glocalization' is the name given to a marital cohabitation that has been obliged to negotiate a bearable modus co-vivendi despite all the sound and fury all too familiar to the majority of wedded couples – as separation, let alone a divorce, is neither realistic nor desirable. Glocalization is the name for a love–hate relationship, mixing attraction with repulsion: love that lusts for proximity, mixed with hate that yearns for distance. That relationship might well have collapsed under the burden of its own incongruity had it not been for a pincer-like duo of inevitabilities: cut off from global supply routes, the place would lack the stuff of which autonomous identities, and the contraptions keeping them alive, are nowadays made; and without the locally improvised and serviced airfields, global forces would have nowhere to land, restaff, replenish and refuel. They are doomed to cohabitation. For better or worse. Till death do them part.